FASSBINDER

W9-DDL-407

WITHDRAWN

FASSBINDER

Peter Iden
Yaak Karsunke
Ruth McCormick
Hans Helmut Prinzler
Wilhelm Roth
Wolfram Schutte
Wilfried Wiegand

*Translated from the German
by Ruth McCormick*

TANAM PRESS   NEW YORK   1981

Translation © 1981 by Tanam Press
Originally published in German as *Fassbinder Reihe Film 2* © 1974
by Carl Hanser Verlag. All rights reserved.

First American edition 1981
For this edition, two new essays have been added to the volume:
*Franz, Mieze, Reinhold, Death and the Devil, Fassbinder's Berlin
Alexanderplatz* by Wolfram Schutte, and *Fassbinder's Reality: an
Imitation of Life* by Ruth McCormick. Both essays © 1981 Tanam
Press

Tanam Press 40 White St. NYC NY 10013

Printed in the USA
ISBN 0-934378-17-7(cloth)
ISBN 0-934378-18-5(paper)

Contents

History of Anti-Teater:
The Beginnings

by Yaak Karsunke

It has been eleven years since the opening of the Action-Theater and ten years since its forced closing, and since then it has become well-known that is was then, on a makeshift stage in a bankrupt B-movie theatre on Munich's Muller-strasse that Fassbinder developed his concept of *anti-teater*. Writing about it today is to follow theatre history, a science which readily brings forth persona and events as monuments to itself to the extent that even clowns must suffer analytic periodizing—early, middle and late Grock. No way, of course, but that's how it goes. Actually, how it went was, for instance, say, on October 3, 1967: at the bar you could get a beer (or a glass of house wine), take it to your seat, and smoke (early Brecht demanded that, but late Brecht never followed it up). Then through the public entrance came a mass of hippies with flowers, who dispersed themselves throughout the audience area, finally scrambling up upon the apron of the stage. Large colored posters covered the walls advertising a series about the Iranian royal couple (four months and one day previously, during a visit by that august pair to West Berlin, a student had been shot by a policeman). The ensemble disappeared behind the adjustable wall, with the exception of a stocky, softspoken young man who fished a handbill out of his jeans, lay himself prone on the stage, took another look at the audience, then opened the pamphlet and read aloud, *"Leonce and Lena.* A comedy by Georg Buchner.''

The comedy which followed was played with gusto, and references to current events were not lacking. When the schoolmaster answered the greeting of the departing vassals with the advice, "Show the proper energy, or energetic measures will be taken,'' there was applause. In view of the Shah, the text became contemporary of its own accord. For the wedding of Leonce and Lena, however, the Action-Theater invoked the Beatles, whose voices over the loud-speaker asked the legitimate question, "Will you still need me, will you still feed me, when I'm sixty-four?"

The provincial critics reacted, if at all, sourly, like nit-picking philologists. For people who had long since taken the finger-thick dust of the Staatstheater on classical texts for the real surface, breathing was a sacrilege; to them, good form with Great Literature consisted in *celebrating* the texts. Nevertheless, the spontaneous-living approach to traditional texts, which was to *play* them, differed even more from what other basement and small theatres were offering. When the large subsidized theatres built their own "basements" with workshops, etc., the mini-theatres reacted for the most part helplessly. There were regressions into theatre history, particularly into Expressionism, with a few standardized Artaud imitations, and production after production of Jarry's sacred *Ubu*. Other than that, the basement theatres only produced amateurish copies of what the official culture industry already offered: Ionesco could be mentioned here, as well as Handke.

The Action-Theater had begun the same way (with *Jacob, or Obedience,* an adaptation of Handke's *Offending the Audience*). Still, there was something more precise, less frivolous and less rigid in the Action-Theater version than in other comparable productions. Only Peer Raben's Living Theatre-like *Antigone,* however, fell clearly outside the handicrafts framework. The director distributed program leaflets which announced, "During the rehearsals texts of individual scenes learned from memory by the actors from various versions were employed spontaneously. The result has been organized by me, supplemented with Brecht's legendary version (of *Antigonemodell 1948* - Y.K.), so that this production is based upon a number of different translations and adaptations." The scenic references were from a more recent date than Old Master Brecht, in whose version it is at one point reported about the citizens of Thebes: "Early in the morning they already stand before the house of Creon. And behind, from out of the battle, at the head of the army against Argos, comes the tyrant, and finds them in front of his house in the half-light of dawn. And leaning on his broadsword, he describes how yonder, in Argos, vultures now hop from corpse to corpse. This gladdens the Thebans, who immediately crown him with laurel.''

Chanted rhythmically by various members of the ensemble, the text could have gone in one ear and out the other; the only remarkable thing was that the same text was repeated again immediately. While the audience was still pondering the meaning of this repetition, the Action introduced a battle scene inspired by ''the rules for hand-to-hand combat used by the German Bundeswehr'' (quite brutal), which was played right into the audience. Then the text was repeated for the third time, and, startled out of the soporific classical rhythms by a dose of Theatre of Cruelty, the audience understood why the Thebans were so gladdened that they crowned their tyrant with laurel.

These proceedings were only approximately denoted through montage or collage. The Action-Theater investigated classical subjects for their intrinsic value, bringing to the stage the collision between the reality of the play and the reality of life. *Iphegenia* came approximately a year later, an elaborately splintered wreck upon the stage, already like an *anti-teater* production directed by Fassbinder. *Antigone* was produced without him; he first came in later, when another member of the group dropped out. By the next production *(Leonce and Lena)*, his name was already listed as one of the four-man directors' collective. Five months (and three premieres) later, he made his debut as a playwright, although still working on unfamiliar ground.

''For Example, Ingolstadt is a freely mounted dramatic reflection upon the psychological world of the middle class as experienced by Marieluise Fleisser. The revised text has been adapted to the language of the original (of *Pioneers in Ingolstadt* -Y.K.). In its associative methods, this production relinquishes historical, philological and dramatic postulates in favor of more complex processes: logic, operating in the cul-de-sac of trivia and missed connections; thinking, not in concepts but in images; talking, not as a formal occurrence but as a mechanism for the repetition of habitual modes of expression.'' Visually, an almost choreographic direction of the

actors corresponded with these concepts, augmented by mimetic references to Catholic ritual. *For Example, Ingolstadt* was, in text and directorial style, a forerunner of *Katzelmacher,* which had its premiere two and a half months later.

On the stage, *Katzelmacher* had a playing time of 40 minutes, while its companion-piece, Jean-Marie Straub's adaptation of Bruckner's *Krankheit der Jugend,* lasted barely 15 minutes. Straub's *Krankheit* was a skeletal but intensely visual critique of Bruckner's commercializing of the problems of youth, to which the director was to return later in his film *The Bridegroom, the Actress and the Pimp.* Evidently because of Straub, the *Suddeutsche Zeitung* for the first time sent, instead of a theatre critic, a film critic to the Action, who also brought more understanding to Fassbinder's work. This seems to confirm the opinion that Fassbinder himself expressed in an interview in 1974: "At first, it was really extreme with me. I produced theatre as if it were film, and directed film as if it were theatre, and did this quite stubbornly."

Obviously "stubborn" in Bavaria meant something different than in Berlin. The (Prussian) observer in 1968, in any case, would have perceived, at any given time, the precise reflection on specific spatial and personal possibilities as pleasant—in this way, the Action-Theater avoided the painful "want to but can't" approach of other small groups. In any case, in the program notes for *Katzelmacher* we find the remark, "Strictly speaking, this should have been a play about older people, but it was to be played by the anti-teater. At the present time, they are all young."

The mention of *"anti-teater"* at this stage was anachronistic, since *Katzelmacher* was still an Action presentation, as was the collective effort, *Axel Caesar Haarmann,* the ensemble's response, at the end of April 1968, to the attempted assassination of Rudi Dutschke. The program leaflet brought to mind the student pamphlets, in form as well as content. "This has to do with Springer...! (and the rotten democracy which allows him to have power)" it said, elucidating with a reference from Brecht, "about what power is, and how it endures as a perverted notion with some people." In response to the beginnings of state repression it was announced that "The net proceeds of all performances will go to the SDS Legal Rights Fund."

Stylistically developed out of the forms of student protest—demonstrations with placques and banners, chants, intervals for teach-ins and sit-ins—*Haarmann* documented the short history of the student movement (chiefly on the Berlin model). At the end, Fassbinder appeared on the stage with a hose, and the "theatre management" announced over the loudspeaker the shutting down of the performance and demanded (naturally, three times) the clearing of the theatre. It was likewise characteristic of the Action-Theater that these words were actually followed by water (which washed the happy smiles off the faces of followers of the "aesthetic Left" quite totally), as was the decision to drop *Haarmann* after a few performances despite good attendance. Since the production had been a quickly improvised reaction to a specific event, it seemed to the ensemble that it was too incomplete for a longer run—at a later time someone would have to look for evidence of a truly new sensibility: Fassbinder was that someone.

The then-current debate about the "death of literature" and the function of cultural work in general, growing out of Marcuse's critical concept of "affirmative culture," was mirrored in the repertory of the Action-Theater in its vigorous pursuit of an ongoing agitprop style *(Chung)*, which would no longer be played in a theatre, but as street theatre, in the framework of the anti-Emergency Powers Act campaign. On Mullerstrasse there was only one direction. On May 21, 1968, in the *Suddeutsche Zeitung*, there appeared a friendly review (those were the days—six years ago!) and a short supplementary notice: "The resumption of *Katzelmacher* and Straub's adaptation of Bruckner's *Krankheit der Jugend* has been postponed indefinitely because the author and leading player of the first piece, Rainer Werner Fassbinder, has been arrested in Paris. It is not clear at this time whether Fassbinder took an active part in the demonstrations or whether he was simply a passing onlooker when he fell into the hands of a police attack squad."

On the same day, the Department for Public Order of the

City of Munich issued a ruling regarding "Execution of City Ordinances for Technical Theatre Management." Investigations by the Technical Control Board had established shortages in certain of the theatre's electrical conduits, and although the Action people had quietly replaced these conduits and got a promise for free repairs from a specialist, the Action-Theater was closed on June 6. During negotiations concerning the closing, an agent of the Department comfortingly explained that the Action-Theater's license would certainly be revoked soon in any case: from the *Chung* reviews it could be concluded that it was without doubt more a question of political cabaret, since the Theatre Licensing Bureau allowed only "predominantly artistic statements." Whether this ordinance was responsible for the re-naming of the Action-Theater is not known, but in July, in any case, the ensemble appeared at the Academy of Visual Arts in Peter Weiss's *Mockinpott* under a new name: "anti-teater = ensemble of the Action-Theater, anti-teater = socialist theatre, anti-teater = information," the program leaflet proclaimed and called, with many blank lines, for further equations.

After the negative experiences which the troupe had had with their attempts at street theatre—"the people don't listen"—they originally wanted to put *Mockinpott* on during breaks for workers in factories. The naivete of this scheme, nevertheless, was a learning experience: the factory owners wouldn't give their permission, and the trade unions gave no support. The troupe avenged themselves with a regression to Jarry: his *Orgie Ubu* was a raging satire on middle-class complacency produced in a basement theatre. The owner, however, would not put up with "political or obscene performances," on his stage, and so, doubly motivated, turned off the lights on the ensemble during a performance. (Because this forced closing, this censorship, took place on a Thursday, in the *anti-teater* production of *The Beggar's Opera* it was later declared, "Thursdays Leopold Bloom went through Dublin. Thursday is a literary day. Thursdays Mackie goes to his whores." But at the time, the *anti-teater* played just about every day but Thursday.)

Finally the group found a home in the back room of an

World on Wires ➤

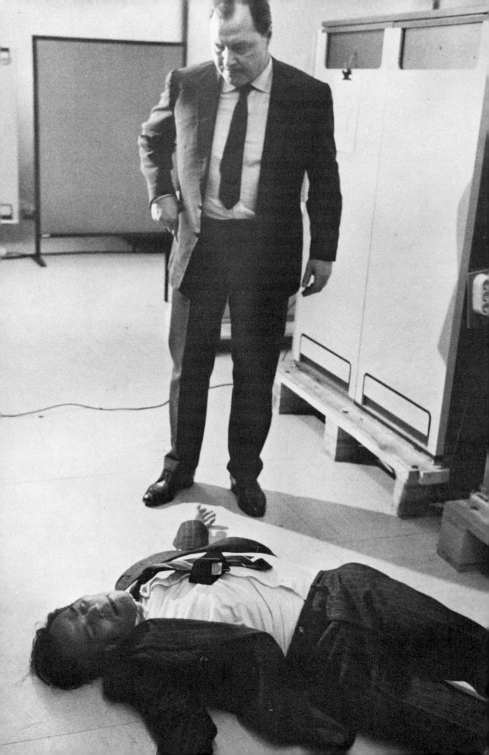

establishment in Schwabing. Their first premiere at the Widow Bolte, on October 25, 1968, was *"Iphegenia on Tauris* by Johann Wolfgang von Goethe,'' adapted and directed by Rainer Werner Fassbinder. In 1962 a Bavarian high school teacher had tried to convince him that *Iphegenia* was ''a drama about the magnanimity of the powerful.'' Within six months, Fassbinder's doubts about this assertion had been realized and confirmed: the so-called ''Easter disturbances'' following the attempted assassination of Dutschke, the May events in Paris, the passing of the Emergency Powers Act, and the intervention of the Warsaw Pact countries in Czechoslovakia were occasions when the powerful had not shown much magnanimity. Fassbinder didn't even bother with the pseudo-Marxist vindication-philology (a la Lukacs perhaps) that tries to pass off classical mendacity as a continuation of humanism, but simply proceeded from the use which bourgeois society makes of supposedly pure poetry: false consciousness about the relations of production, and propaganda for the status quo.

Fassbinder's *Iphegenia* sits in a Hollywood-style swinging cage made of tubing and wire netting—a redheaded decoy bird who sings the affirmative airs of Goethe (set to music by Peer Raben), with which she entices two young homosexuals, Orestes and Pylades. Their dialogues with King Thoas overflow before long into the words of the altercation between Fritz Teufel and Rainer Langhans and City Magistrate Schwerdtner during the Westberliner Kommune trial: a reading of the list of prison terms given out during the political trials of student demonstrators followed. Visual quotes from comic strips and Living Theatre were likewise inserted into the action, as were quotes from Mao and Paul McCartney. Although the play was presented in an otherwise traditional way, Fassbinder deleted all the things that he felt should now be forgotten.

In the course of the evening, even some of the advocates of the ''anarchist'' wing of Munich SDS came to understand this, though at first they tried to disrupt the performance, because to them theatre still only seemed justified—if at all—as agitprop (and because they were numerically too weak to articulate this view in a large theatre.) If Alfons

Scharf is correct in his thesis that the anti-authoritarian movement can be understood as a latter-day cultural-revolutionary extension of the failed bourgeois revolution of 1848 *(Answers of an Educated Worker* - Guide 25), then Fassbinder was quite a bit in advance of his opponents that evening. His first reaction to the disintegration and fragmentation, or "dogmatization," of the former Extra-Parliamentary Opposition consisted in a theatrical reflection upon the traditional cultural foundations of its supporters: Fassbinder followed *Iphegenia* with an adaptation of *Ajax* by Sophocles, under the motto, "What's most important, it seems to me, is to create discomfort for the institutions of the bourgeoisie."

Nevertheless, the (compared to *Iphegenia*) much-older *Ajax* resisted Fassbinder's re-working. The chronological distance between the two plays played a part in the subsequently different traditions to which they belonged and functions they had served in the socialization of German middle-class school children. For this reason the suspicion of ideology was justified—in *Ajax*, Menelaos says, "Surely it's a bad citizen who, as a citizen, disdains to heed the words of the rulers." —and the shifting of the action from antiquity to a *Bundeswehr* officers' club was so unconvincing that the modernization remained cabaret. In his adaptation of *The Beggar's Opera* (Gay-Pepuch), Fassbinder again borrowed only the characters and the staging, supplementing it with his own experiences with the Munich subculture and commune-dwellers, but still, not all the conflicts between the original and the modern adaptation could be fruitfully solved—Fassbinder's second original play was more successful. *Preparadise, Sorry Now* was a very rigorous and symmetrically conceived production about "basically fascistic attitudes in everyday life," alternating dialogues between, and stories about, Ian Brady and Myra Hinley (the British "moor murderers"), augmented with "textual recollections on liturgical and cult cannibalism." Fassbinder's work, like Bunuel's, showed stylistic traces of a Catholic environment. Once again, one could discern the minimal, clearly-defined movements and gestures that were this group's version of the Brechtian "alienation-effect", which even at this point afforded formal support to inexperienced actors without needlessly confining the "superstars" (like Hanna Schygulla). We can read the script of the play (along with *Katzelmacher* and *The Beggar's Opera*) in the first volume of *anti-teater* plays published by Suhrkamp, and see that there are possible variations in the order of individual scenes because "we can put the play together for ourselves, as we see fit, although the "connections between the different complexes should be followed." The looseness of this formulation should still not digress from considerations of form and content: this was also typical of anti-teater.

Ironically, with *Anarchy in Bavaria,* the group crossed over for the first time to subsidized ground, during the Week of Theatre Workshops, to which the small theatre groups of Munich were invited. Fassbinder accepted the invitation, and the reviewer who missed this performance because of private anarchy missed the final separation of anti-teater from its "subculture" period. Since then, there has been a wager circulating as to whether or not Fassbinder and his ensemble would become corrupted and integrated—"Take part in human endeavors, judge the fighting form of the opponent impartially, and fight for your interests to the finish" (Brecht).

KATZELMACHER
Ein Film von Rainer Werner Fassbinder

The Impact-Maker

By Peter Iden

The program with which Rainer Werner Fassbinder made the transition from the milieu of Munich's basement theatres to the big stage and bigger audiences of a state theatre was called a "showdown" by the *Bremer Helfer.* On a windy day in early November, 1969, the Bremer Theater showed two of Fassbinder's films, *Katzelmacher* and *Love Is Colder than Death,* and two theatrical works, his version of Goldoni's *The Coffeehouse* and the cabaret-style review, *Anarchy in Bavaria.* Fassbinder's talents became forcefully apparent that day; seldom had so much promising material by one artist been seen all at once. Everything was anarchic, from the staccato tempo and accentuated artifice of the Goldoni piece to Fassbinder himself, who was almost stupidly inarticulate in a discussion afterwards, hardly capable of uttering a word. Still, it was clear that here was a talent to be reckoned with. With each new theatrical work Fassbinder has presented since then, the certainty with which he was accepted in Bremen at that time is once again thrown into doubt. This makes the search for an overview of his work difficult at this point. In retrospect, what seemed like a beginning in Bremen has not developed as might have been expected; rather, what has actually followed has been one new beginning after another. Any survey of his work has to take into account the fact that there is no continuous principle to be discovered. No system of related reflections on Fassbinder's theatre can be established right now.

This "showdown," a chapter in the life and productive activity of a writer-director who was twenty-three years old when he came to Bremen also marked a milestone, a new beginning, for Kurt Hubner's Bremer Theater. It was the penultimate of a series of events—the last being the debut of set designer Wilfried Minks as a director—relating to Hubner's work in Bremen. Hubner had discovered Fassbinder at the *anti-teater* in Munich (he saw *The Beggar's Opera*).

The techniques Fassbinder used with his group of young actors in that basement theatre were still in evidence in the Bremen production of *The Coffee House*, and earned for the troupe entry into the theatrical establishment, first in Bremen, then in Bochum, although not without conflicts. (To put it one way, the entry in Bochum was followed shortly thereafter by a rather violent exit.) What characterized the style of Fassbinder and his group? A great spontaneity in acting, an inclination to establish the choice of material arbitrarily, serendipity and nonchalance with regard to staging, but also, a vehement joy and a relaxed, lighthearted kind of aggressiveness. Fassbinder's place in German theatre is still defined by these features, even as he himself moves farther and farther away from the group.

But isn't Fassbinder's theatrical style merely a sidetrack in his general artistic development? A survey of his activities after he left Bremen shows a distinct preponderance of works for film and television. Invariably, there have been crossovers between theatre and film: plays like *The Bitter Tears of Petra von Kant* and *Bremen Freedom* have been done in both media. But the number of theatrical productions has been considerably less than that of the film projects. We should proceed with caution, however, before coming to the conclusion that Fassbinder prefers film to theatre. He turns back to the theatre again and again—and again and again he is frustrated by the built-in limitations it puts on his work. These difficulties with theatre have not caused him to abandon his ongoing theatrical work, because in his view, it is theatre rather than film which offers the greater possibility for control over the productive means and their further development. This may well be the reason for the decision, in the fall of 1974, to take over the Frankfurt TAT (Theater am Turm).

What is conspicuous in the body of his films is also noticeable in his theatrical works to date: an overflowing talent; a passion of work that borders on self-destruction; confusion—but also the energy to vary his subject-matter, style and aesthetic position at will. In the notebook for the adaptation of Lope de Vega's *The Burning Village*, we can read the datelines Munich, Madrid, Fuerteventura, Las

Palmas and Paris as an indication of the restless mobility of the author, who is always somewhere other than (though not necessarily farther than) his audience. So we see that Fassbinder's theatrical undertakings, in the sense of being an "oeuvre," cannot be described as a unified whole, but rather, appear as a series of disparate statements. These productions have usually been thrown together at short notice, under great pressure, and with minimal time for preparation. There are wild stories about the genesis of these plays and performances—faulty planning and subsequently incomplete realizations—and whoever talks about Fassbinder and the theatre must take these elements into account. Each announcement of a new project brought a surprise. The schedule listed titles of plays that had not yet been written (for example, *The Gentle Tangos of the Fascists* on the Frankfurt programme). Adaptations were presented in which it was plain to see—and Fassbinder readily admitted it—that the author had barely read the original *(The Coffeehouse, The Burning Village)*. Such dubious carryings-on didn't hurt the appeal or success of Fassbinder's plays—in fact, quite the reverse. Their success was based upon Fassbinder's endless need for self-expression, but also at least as much upon the demand for novelty which prevailed in the theatre in the late Sixties and early Seventies. Favored by the shortage of playwrights and the difficulty writers for the theatre were experiencing in dealing with contemporary issues, Fassbinder's plays opened in Bremen, in Bochum, in Nuremburg, in Frankfurt and in Berlin. These premieres were eagerly-awaited events, but the tense expectation was often followed by disappointment and complaints. With the unique exception of his *Bremen Freedom* (a "real" drama), Fassbinder's plays have consistently had a strong impact on the German theatre. He produced them quickly, and the night they opened, he had already moved on to something else. It was Fassbinder's good luck that the German theatre couldn't get along without his plays. He threw himself into them, and then just as quickly dropped them.

Since the particulars of these dramatic incursions into the marketplace are not united by any common factors, we can only characterize Fassbinder's work in the theatre by sketching in a (incomplete and willy-nilly) selection of examples. The discontinuity of these works makes any reconstruction of their connections impossible. Therefore, we will consider five examples: *The Coffeehouse* (Bremen, end of 1969), *The Burning Village* (Bremen, end of 1970), *Blood on the Cat's Collar* (Nuremburg, March 1971), *The Bitter Tears of Petra von Kant* (Frankfurt "Experimenta," June 1971) and *Bremen Freedom* (Bremen, December 1971). All were done within a period of just three years. More recent works, up to the adaptation of Ibsen's *Hedda Gabler* in Berlin early in 1974 (allowing for the consequences of the run-in with Peter Zadek in Bochum) have not really gone beyond or added anything significantly new to what can be found in the works discussed below. Fassbinder wrote three of the selected plays himself *(Blood on the Cat's Collar, The Bitter Tears of Petra von Kant* and *Bremen Freedom); two* are adaptations *(The Coffeehouse* and *The Burning Village); three (Coffeehouse, Cat's Collar* and *Bremer Freiheit)* he directed himself, while the other two were directed by Peer Raben under his guidance. In one, *Blood on the Cat's Collar,* the author-director also played a role. The most obvious external connection between these plays is the fact that actors from the old *anti-teater* could still be seen in them; Margit Carstensen, whom Fassbinder had discovered in the Bremen ensemble, was a regular from *Blood on the Cat's Collar* on. Here are five specimens from the work of one of the most productive talents in the German theatre in recent years—examples of the many-sided abilities, but also, the many-sided weaknesses, of Rainer Werner Fassbinder. Now, a quick trip through some of these endeavors.

1. *The Coffeehouse, or Games from other Games (Das Kaffeehaus).*

In Fassbinder's treatment of this old (1750) Goldoni comedy, we can discern for the first time something that will subsequently often characterize his adaptations of material from other sources: the substitution of one reality for another, which is itself in turn stamped by a composite of elements of widely differing value. Goldoni's play, in which Don Marzio, an irksome, parasitical chatterbox and gossip, is eventually forced to leave Venice, concerns the slandering

The Coffeehouse

of the character and the society which produced him—one in which love and financial affairs are inextricably intertwined. Fassbinder retains the social definition of the characters (except for the servant Trappolo, who becomes an interesting figure of contrast), and makes of Don Marzio a sad, almost Schnitzleresque character, whose melancholy and morbidity form the center of the piece. The set, which was designed by Wilfried Minks, invokes the backdrops for Peter Stein's version of *Tasso*, produced at the same theatre: now, there is a rose-colored carpet, a tall glass structure with a dummy of a cake on top, and to the left and right, as erotic *apercus,* male and female nude statues. All the actors are always on the stage, moving between black chairs in handsome costumes, but, amid all this opulence, barefoot with Colt revolvers on their hips. Venice and a Western saloon. Images as syntheses of images. The direction is very slow. Everything is projected as if out of a deep paralysis; the characters glide into one another, creep around each other, lose their way, in little games of the changing of an attitude, a gentle motion, a vague remembrance. Fassbinder has borrowed movements and gestures from Peter Stein's *Tasso*, settings from his own and Straub's films, and mannerisms from Gary Cooper and Bruno Ganz. In the female roles, Brigitte Janner and Margit Carstensen are reminiscent of Jutta Lampe and Edith Clever. If it can be said be said that Stein, in his *Tasso* at the same theatre, used mannerisms in his play to define it more clearly for his actors, in Fassbinder's play the mannerisms no longer retain their critical perspective. Everything in this adaptation consists of games from other games; it is a production of other productions.

2. *The Burning Village*, or *Revolt as an Obscene Gesture (Das Brennende Dorf)*.

This evening also—Peer Raben is directing—disintegrates into moments of loud conflict. In Lope de Vega's play, King Ferdinand leaves the village of Fuente Ovejuna in the hands of an overlord. The lord rules harshly; when he kidnaps a young woman who has refused him, the villagers kill him shortly before the wedding. Ferdinand, the king, holds a trial, but finds no single party guilty; when he asks who killed the lord, everyone responds, but only with the name of the village. Impressed with the solidarity of the villagers, the king absolves them all from punishment.

This happy ending, in which the clemency of the ruler is extolled, is changed in Fassbinder's version. The peasants are commanded by Ferdinand to attend a great feast, after which he intends to hang them. Instead, the accused drag the king, the queen and their entourage from the throne and make a meal of them.

This final action of the bloodthirsty mob was foreshadowed earlier in the play. The killing of the lord (whom Fassbinder calls the Commander), planned and carried out by the women of the village, ends in a bloodbath. The women fall upon the man, bury him under their bodies, tear him apart, and are then seen covered with his blood, rolling around on the ground. This signifies that these rebels, who eat their oppressor, have become beasts—in fact, were beasts from the very beginning. The girl Laurentia, whom the Commander later kidnaps, intimates this development in her first scene, when she describes a dish she's cooked that tastes like human flesh. Thus we find in Fassbinder's adaptation numerous examples of the connection which exists in his view between sexuality and violence, desire and frenzy, rebellion and sensuality. The women praise the Commander's powerful genitals. When they kill him, we suspect that this is not just an act of rebellion against despotism and terror, but more, an enormous collective orgasm. This is the socially untenable position of this production—that it understands the peasants' struggle for liberation only as a release of their sexual energy. Once again social relations and motivations are displaced by perverse forms, such as frenzy and orgiastic mindlessness.

3. *Blood on the Cat's Collar,* or *It's a Shame about People (Blut am Hals der Katze).*

After these adaptations, Fassbinder directed a play of his own. Phoebe Zeitgeist, the always-naked and constantly-subjected-to-terrible-tortures title character of the famous American comicstrip, moves through the play like a double of Indra's daughter in Strindberg's *Dream Play.* She reflects upon what the other characters do and say, and tries, as if she were from a distant star, to discover what linguistic and gestural conventions people use to communicate with each other. In the last third of the play, she thinks she's succeeded in mastering them, and attempts to return the words and motions she's picked up to the characters from whom she's learned them. However, Phoebe has only heard sounds and learned gestures, so she can only give them back by rote; to a gesture of affection, she adds a sentence conveying hatred. The learning process of the alien remains incomplete; her reactions become displaced, de-ranged. The irritation this state of affairs causes the other characters eventually coagulates all their actions. Phoebe, who has demonstrated that their forms of communication are malfunctioning, paralyzes the vital nerve of their environment.

The play suggests that we almost always learn the wrong thing; the lamentable condition of the world is just what it is—all we can do is put up with it. So there's a lot of complaining in this play. The anti-teater production, directed by Fassbinder (who also appears on the stage as a character hanging out in a bar), was commissioned for a theatre in Nuremburg. The production conveyed a studied nonchalance, a pretty, soft calmness of expression. Beautiful females and macho-looking males moved as if in a trance, an enigmatic dance. These sequences emitted a strange, enticing perfume, a hint of longing, the roar of heavy motorcycles, wild adventures followed by weary depressions, crooks in the courtyard and small talk at pimps' cocktail parties. The value of the production lay in such slim vague attractions. Fassbinder's attempt to deal with the unreliability of the forms of social discourse puts him in the company of Gombrowicz and Handke. However, his play lacks the poetic strength of Gombrowicz and the cool analysis of Handke. Here, Fassbinder's theatre is static and lacking in perspective. He sketches a portrait of sickness, but as a representation of symptoms, not an explanation of causes.

4. *The Bitter Tears of Petra von Kant,* or *True Feeling (Die Bitteren Tranen der Petra von Kant).*

This original work, written at the request of the founders of the fourth "Experimenta" and produced by Peer Raben in Darmstadt for a Frankfurt opening, was later to become a film directed by the author. (For a description of the film, see Wilhelm Roth's filmography later in this book.)

In the theatrical version, Fassbinder was looking for a new beginning. It starts with the question, "How much and by what theatrical means can the reality of feelings (love, jealousy, hatred) be represented?" As an answer to this question, we are presented with the glossy-magazine world of a sophisticated lesbian fashion designer (Fassbinder had Margit Carstensen in mind for this role from the beginning) who is separated from her lover as a frame of reference and at the same time, as an existing reality. The play then forgets its original proposition, in that feelings are only represented as excessive sentimentality, and becomes pathetic. However, all appearances aside, this is Fassbinder's most urgent attempt to deal with other things than purely artistic realities.

5. *Bremen Freedom,* or *Live and Let Die (Bremer Freiheit).*

The Bitter Tears of Petra von Kant can be seen as an effort to develop hackneyed, trivial material to such an extent that it becomes something that is often encountered in Fassbinder's plays and adaptations: the trial of the credibility or falsehood of the pathetically stylized figure on the stage.

Bremen Freedom, the original production of which he directed himself in Bremen, now extends this trial of the validity of strong feelings, weighty gestures and decisive action into its most difficult phase—that of tragedy. The play takes its subject from a 19th century account of a certain "beautiful Gesina," a famous poisoner. The treatment of this subject has its literary-historical point of reference in another play, which was written around the same time (as the reports on Gesina), Hebbel's *Mary Magdalene*. Like the young woman Klara in Hebbel's play, Geesche Gottfried in *Bremen Freedom* experiences the world as a place without freedom, a place of oppression under a system of rigid bourgeois values which allows a women no life of her own. In both plays, the father represents this system. Hebbel permits his Master Anton, in the end, to suspect this murderous order of which he himself is a representative; the man loses his grip on the world. Where Hebbel leaves off (with doubts, questioning the old order), Fassbinder begins. His Geesche doesn't accept her lack of freedom, and frees herself, little by little, murder by murder. Her first words in the Bremen production are, "And me?" The words are a declaration: this is someone in a ferment, beginning to think about herself.

And beginning to do something for herself. Before long, this woman will take action against the things that oppress her: we now see how those who are guilty will die. Her husband, who orders her about and humiliates her in front of friends; her children, for whose sake she had decided not to marry another man; then the other man himself; later, someone who endangers her business, a cousin, a brother, and finally even a female friend—they all get arsenic in their teacups, and none of them outlive the scene in which they first appear. But the elimination of constraints is always only temporary; the oppressor keeps coming back. As the creditor who demands the money she borrowed meets his end, her brother, who only wants to belittle her, waits in the wings. Finally, when the murderess is discovered, she says, "Now, I'll die," and sings again the pious little song with which she accompanied each murder.

What was the purpose of this reworking of Hebbel's bourgeois tragedy as a drama of liberation? The title, *Bremen*

Freedom, embodies a double cynicism: freedom is not what Geesche gets, nor is it what she was so murderously after. It is possible to notice a tendency here which is critical of contemporary revolutionary praxis. Not only is Geesche's subjugation, so to speak, an expression of social disproportion but the way in which she pursues her ideal of liberation, in the process perverting it, is also "wrong". Fassbinder's production does not elaborate upon this political aspect: it is more concerned with the esthetic problems of the staging than with the social dimension of the subject. Fassbinder, Margit Carstensen (who played Geesche) and set designer Minks were examining the possibility of bringing together different planes of reality within the context of a theatrical presentation. Minks supplied the symbolic level: at the Concordia (the Bremen studio-theatre where the play opened), a dark, horizontal cross formed the playing area. This cross was surrounded by red plastic carpeting, upon which several pieces of furniture—the buffet with the poison, a sofa, a dressing table—drifted as if upon a sea (of blood?). Gray Hitchcockian seagulls were painted on the walls, and the audience area was decorated with portholes and galleons, like a ship. This conveyed a very emphatic image: the cross represented the "old order," which was "at sea." With regard to acting style, Fassbinder and Carstensen decided upon a formal transition from cold realism to mannered sly gestures in which feelings of love, longing and suffering were expressèd, as well as a flickering, anarchic sensation of joy after every murder.

End of trip. What conclusions can we make? Fassbinder's career as a theatrical director and playwright has always also been a journey through old subjects and dramatic (and cinematic) forms. A journey and a crossing: it seems sometimes as if Fassbinder's work draws its impetus from a fascination with things already discovered or remembered, as much as from a desire to shatter them in order to create a place for his own ideas, within the context of the old. The examples above bear witness to his attempts to define himself both in terms of his own inner experiences and his environment. Of course, we also have to deal with his self-references, which proceed from his (very important for theatre) personal interventions into historical continuity. Reality, past and present, is transformed. Artistic ersatz-reality is substituted. It has often been exciting to witness this substitution. But then again, we can see in these works a great sacrifice of reality. If Fassbinder really wants to intensify his theatrical work in Frankfurt, he will have to apply himself to elements which he has avoided up until now. He must look at reality, and faced with it, stand firm. Then, the diffusness of his past works will come together as an indication of things to come—a prologue.

P. S. April, 1975

A year has passed. But the prologue still goes on. In the meantime, Fassbinder has taken over the Frankfurt TAT. He began his work in Frankfurt with a production of the Yaak Karsunke adaptation of Zola's *Germinal.* His direction was almost friendly, softening the social impact of the novel: Zola's gesture of accusation was turned into a melodrama.

Fassbinder then played the porter Jean in Strindberg's *Miss Julie* (with Margit Carstensen as Julie). It was a precarious collective production—unsteady: and Fassbinder's acting was so weak that the character became weak. We have previously noted that a tendency toward self-representation can be perceived as a characteristic of Fassbinder's theatrical work. In Frankfurt, the catchword was now "finding himself." In the meantime, after a few months the ensemble almost fell apart. Fassbinder's production of Chekhov's *Uncle Vanya,* though lovingly attempted by the director and his actors, deteriorated into mournful melodrama. This may well have been because of these diffused efforts at self-discovery.

P.S.

Fassbinder left the TAT in 1975. Is he finished with the theatre?

The Doll in the Doll
Observations on Fassbinder's Films

by Wilfried Wiegand

In 1974, Fassbinder celebrated his twenty-eighth birthday. In the past five years he had made twenty feature films, not counting the seven episodes of his two television series. He also wrote (or at least co-authored) the scripts for all these films, and acted in several of them, as well as in films by other directors. He has continued almost without pause with his work in the theatre, and still does radio plays. In short, Fassbinder is more productive than any other German film director. Why is he so productive?

Development

Until three years ago, however, Fassbinder's style showed very little development. The already-established "Fassbinder-style," of which *Katzelmacher* is perhaps the most popular example, was considered for a while to be his ultimate achievement. Characteristics of this style can still be discerned in his depiction of an artificial world of bourgeois decadence, as in *Whity* and *The Bitter Tears of Petra von Kant,* or in *Jail Bait,* where he creates a lower-class environment through his earlier, more naturalistic methods. In any case, since *Merchant of the Four Seasons,* Fassbinder has constantly borrowed from different film genres, employing new forms of expression alongside his earlier stylistic devices. Now, a new kind of work has appeared, which might be termed socially committed popular art, which he initiated with *Merchant of the Four Seasons* and has continued with the television series *Eight Hours are Not a Day* and the film *Ali: Fear Eats the Soul.* With the unique exception of Volker Schlondorff's *Mord und Totschlag (Murder and Homicide),* Fassbinder's films *Welt am Draht (World on Wires)* and *Martha* are closer to the Hollywood model than those of any other German director since Fritz Lang.

◄ *Effi Briest*

It would seem necessary, therefore, to understand Fassbinder's stylistic development as being linear, from simple beginnings to always more complex formulations. However, such an interpretation would do only very superficial justice to his particular development, which is, rather, spasmodic, moving not only forward but backward, seeking its potential not only in the future but in the past. For this reason we would search in vain in *Effi Briest* for signs of the Hollywood techniques that otherwise characterize Fassbinder's more recent films. On the contrary, *Effi* is more closely related to that Dreyer-Bresson-Straub tradition which has more to do with Fassbinder's beginnings than with his later work.

Because of these recapitulations and self-quotes, the use of the same speech patterns and actors, and even the repetition of musical motifs. we become increasingly aware that in each one of his new films we are rediscovering something that we have already seen in one of his earlier ones. It becomes apparent that in spite of new themes and stylistic advances, Fassbinder fundamentally always seems to concern himself with the same problems, which never lose their importance for him, but only reappear in new forms. This may be another reason why Fassbinder is so productive.

Despair

Perhaps Straub even had this in mind when he said that Fassbinder's short films were "films which have to do, above all, with the violence, as such, of the Germans."[1] These films function violently, indeed, because not only are people threatened by guns in them, but also because there is considerable aggression against the audience. It becomes apparent here that Fassbinder has no intention of concealing the meagerness of his production, which has been dictated by financial restrictions, but rather, displays an almost amateurish directness. The form of the narrative is established on the same aesthetic level as the events with which it deals. No mediating artistic devices are thrust between the observer and the observed, with the result that the poverty of the observer is blatantly suggested. Fassbinder's first full-length films are

Why Does Herr R Run Amok?

also examples of this *ars povera.* In *Love Is Colder than Death,* for example, the office of the syndicate consists of one room which can be seen, on the one hand, as a place where authority is supposedly exercised, while on the other, the desk, the bowl which sits upon it, and the draperies behind it are so shabby that the spectator experiences the whole arrangement as a disturbing contradiction between what should be seen and what is actually there.

Fassbinder has stressed that this poverty makes his films more honest than those of other German directors. "The only thing that bothers me about *48 Hours to Acapulco* (Klaus Lemke) is that the women are too chic and the highways are too elegant... in my films the characters are established in a story that is just as tacky as they are, whereas (Rudolf) Thome always thinks he has to make his characters more elegant than his stories."[2] It is precisely this comparison with Thome (particularly his film *Detective,* which was released before Fassbinder's first feature) which makes the determining distinction evident: in Thome's film people certainly also die violently, but there is no inkling of the suffering that characterizes almost all of Fassbinder's work. With the semi-exception of *Rio das Mortes,* we find no comedy in his films. Instead, there are outbreaks of despair—something that does not happen in the works of other contemporary German directors. One such sequence ends *The American Soldier,* when Ricky's brother throws himself on his corpse; another occurs when the title character in *The Bitter Tears of Petra von Kant* confesses that she isn't "crazy" about Karen, but "I love her... I love her as I have never loved anyone in my life." Absolute despair asserts itself when Hans drinks himself to death in *Merchant of the Four Seasons,* while his wife and best friend look on, and when Kurt Raab kills his wife, child and a neighbor and then hangs himself in *Why Does Herr R Run Amok?* One would have to look far back into the history of German cinema to find comparisons. The observation made by the production manager in *Beware of a Holy Whore*—"You know, the only thing I accept is despair"—could be a key to Fassbinder's work. The actor who plays the production manager is Rainer Werner Fassbinder.

Peepshow Space

Typical of Fassbinder's style is a kind of staging which could accurately be described as having derived from the peepshow, where the deepest boundary is a wall parallel to the camera. Again and again we will see a sparsely furnished set, in which a rectangular table stands diagonal to the wall. People sit behind and at the sides of the table, while the side facing the audience remains empty, as in Leonardo's *Last Supper.* Fassbinder also often uses this arrangement for outdoor sequences. It is not by accident that certain dramatically decisive exterior scenes take place in courtyards. In *American Soldier* and *Merchant of the Four Seasons* the walls of the buildings surround the characters like the walls of a room. It is not by accident either that landscapes play a very small role in his films. Two exceptions are *Niklashauser Fahrt* and *Effi Briest,* which are, significantly, his only historical films: here, the landscape takes on greater significance, just as it played a larger part in the lives of people of earlier times. Consequently, Fassbinder deliberately places the people of our own time into more constricted surroundings.

Since *Beware of a Holy Whore,* Fassbinder has demonstrated even more complicated fields of vision. In the very important table sequences, for example, the table is no longer placed diagonally, but seems to take refuge vertically in the depth of the frame (as in the scene in which Hans drinks himself to death in *Merchant of the Four Seasons*). The space in such sequences has acquired more depth, and the camera now requires minimal movement to convey to the spectator an emotional dimension of depth that was lacking in the more distanced "Last Supper" construction. In the more recent films this stereoscopic effect is often employed in such a way that, for example, in the science-fiction world of *Welt am Draht,* the room (through use of a wide-angle lens) seems to contract itself like a tube, as if the spectator were looking through the wrong end of a telescope: the room appears larger and the people inside it become strangers in their own world. Or in *Fear Eats the Soul,* when Ali takes leave of Emmi, telling her he wants "to be alone for a while," we see Emmi through the corridor, standing in the kitchen, far removed from us. Space and perspective interpret the characters, as do the few outdoor sequences, of which the most explicit is perhaps the one shot from the airplane in *Gods of the Plague* where we see the hero's automobile very small in the middle of the landscape—an image of freedom that the occupants of the car may possibly sense, but cannot see as clearly as we can.

Sound effects and Music

The closeup of the swirling coffee in the cup in the fourth part of *Eight Hours Are Not a Day* is symbolic (although not, as in Godard's famous scene in *Two or Three Things I Know about Her,* as a metaphor for the universe), but only in the sense that it reflects the stirred-up feelings of the character. Many sounds are also symbolic: a seagull shrieks at precisely the moment when the heroine of *Martha* confides to her friend during the course of a boat trip that she is afraid of her husband, and in *Effi Briest* an owl's cry and a foghorn tell us what the heroine does not dare to say.

Even the music, with its repeated motifs of melancholy, tenderness, tension and stress, interprets what is going on in such a way that it expresses the feelings of the characters. This is equally true of the sound effects.

Accordingly, the sound in *Welt am Draht* is intentionally "slightly attenuated" (Fassbinder), as is almost always the case when a film is post-synced. The director considers this important "to some extent, to create sound effects which are like direct sound or even more pronounced than direct sound... so that it will become clearer, through something artificial, something introduced into the sound, because direct sound is really only a by-product of the original sound." (Fassbinder.) Especially in *Gods of the Plague,* we find this exaggerated use of natural sound in the deafening clatter of glass and rattling of spoons, and in *Love Is Colder than Death,* in the scene in which Bruno lies on the bed waiting for Joanna to get undressed, we hear from the offspace the opening of a zipper with the same clarity with which the hero must hear it.

Camera Movements

In Fassbinder's more recent films, the camera functions to show how the characters in question perceive their surroundings. The table shots, for example, may now be set up crosswise, and we now see figures in the foreground with their backs to us, cut off by the edge of the frame. By the same token, with this handling of space the camera no longer remains adjusted parallel to the action nor travels along with it, but executes complex movements from a depth perspective. Beginning with *Beware of a Holy Whore,* we have camera movements which take in the total dimensions of a room, not simply by following a circular pattern, but by creeping zig-zag into each corner of the room. The scenes in the hotel lobby in *Beware* and the tavern sequences in *Pioneers in Ingolstadt* are examples, as is the wedding party scene in the fourth part of *Eight Hours Are Not a Day,* of this technique, where the camera allows us to look from the corridor into diverse rooms in a building. Even the characters move in more complicated patterns. The scenes in which characters sitting on barstools turn abruptly toward or away from their neighbors are perhaps most significant in this respect. If we compare this manipulation of space in his more recent films with the elementary camera movements we see in *Katzelmacher* (the almost stationary camera, the rigid movements of the characters), the visual space now seems better able to accomodate the feelings of the characters. Now there is space for human experience.

Closeups

In his more recent films, Fassbinder has begun to use closeups, something he seldom did earlier. Since *Merchant of the Four Seasons,* closeups have served to define highly dramatic moments. In this film, we see a closeup of broken dishes when the two former Legion buddies meet again; we also see at close range the hands of the prostitute as she unfastens her blouse at the police station and the faces of the adversaries in the scene in the kitchen when Hans confronts his business partner with evidence of the latter's duplicity. Since *Whity,* Fassbinder has used the kind of closeup traditionally employed in Hollywood films to throw the viewer off the track: in the opening scene, a doorknob turns ominously, and the mother cries out in fear, but it's only Whity who steps into the room. Similarly, in *Martha,* at one point the telephone is foregrounded in such a way that it dominates the whole room, thus taking on the same importance in the frame that it has at this moment for Martha in the story. In the fifth part of *Eight Hours Are Not a Day,* we watch with the eyes of the jealous Manfred the window behind which Monika turns out the light. This principle is applied consistently in *Martha.* The interior of the house seems more lofty than it is in reality because the dramatic significance of the staircase imparts to the room a dimension of height that it objectively lacks. Actually, the plot of the film can be interpreted as "Martha's vision." In the entire picture, there is hardly a shot that is not set up to show us what Martha is experiencing. In this respect, the psychological dimension is no longer conveyed by the kind of "red herring" devices mentioned above: Fassbinder has found the means to tell a story from the point of view of a character.

Toward a More Complex Style

In any case, Fassbinder has not relinquished the alienation effects of the earlier films in his more recent works. His table shots are now, to be sure, constructed along much more complex lines, but he often collapses old solutions into the new. For example, in the final scene of the fifth part of *Eight Hours Are Not a Day,* when Grandma sits beside Gregor and both look straight ahead at the door behind which Monika encounters Manfred, we experience all at once how symmetrical (that is, solemn) the scene is for the characters themselves, and how lively and colorful (and humorous) it is for us. The shot (in *Fear Eats the Soul*) in which Emmi and Ali celebrate their wedding in the restaurant shows the two framed so symmetrically by the doorway that, on the one hand, the isolation they feel becomes obvious, and on the other, this frame-within-a-frame reveals the relationship in which we stand to the characters. At the same time, through the same stylistic device, we are made aware that the couple is lonely and vulnerable, but that they are also prototypes of ourselves. This is a dialectical use of style, which portrays reality with all its contradictions. It follows that to some extent, Fassbinder makes wider use of the simple solutions of his earlier style. The wedding table sequences in *Martha* are composed along the same parallel lines as similar sequences in his early films. What is new here, of course, in *Martha,* is the way production values are employed with regard to these basic compositions. Just as the language in Fassbinder's films ranges from hesitant, stammering subjective confessions to aphoristic formulations of objective perception, his visual mode of expression has now become much richer: it includes everything from extremely subjective closeups of details to paradigmatic constructions that function like visual aphorisms.

Prison-worlds

Fassbinder's characters live in the rooms of his films as one might live in a prison. Already in his 1966 short film *Das Kleine Chaos (The Small Chaos)* a living room is virtually transformed into a jail for a woman after a gang invades her home. The opening sequences of *Love Is Colder than Death* takes place in the prison of a gangster syndicate, and the manor house in *Whity* becomes a kind of jail due to the use of color composition, wood panelling and floral decoration. A prisonlike atmosphere characterizes the proletarian/petty bourgeois homes in *Katzelmacher, Jail Bait* and *Merchant of the Four Seasons,* and Herr R lives in a kind of prison in *Why Does Herr R Run Amok?* When Herr R finally hangs himself, his behavior is similar to that of Hans at the end of *Merchant of the Four Seasons* when he drinks himself to death: psychic explosions often become inevitable after the possibilities for the development of an individual become stifled by narrow, claustrophobic spaces. The same is true of aggression, which bursts forth in *Katzelmacher* even though the characters are seldom closed up in rooms. The space which encloses them is defined by their ever-recurring patterns of speech and movement. This is the prison of provincial life. These people seem to be kept at a distance from any possibility for a full or beautiful life by invisible iron bars. This even happens to members of the upper classes like Effi Briest, Nora Helmer and Petra von Kant. Fassbinder has drawn prisons of a different kind in *The Bitter Tears of Petra von Kant* and *Welt am Draht.* Here, people live like exotic fish in an aquarium. In many of his films, he uses potted palms and floral arrangements to achieve this effect in his rooms. We inspect the characters, moreover, as if through a glass wall, which they themselves appear not to notice, until one day some of them look out and suspect that out there, on the other side of the pane, true, real life must exist. At times, Fassbinder portrays life in a glass house quite directly, as in the final scene of *Welt am Draht*, or when Martha must go out to the veranda when she wants to smoke a cigarette, or in the closing shot of *Merchant of the Four Seasons*, which is photographed from outside the window of a Volkswagen bus. In *Beware of a Holy Whore*, a connection is made between a feeling of distance from real life and the artist (Fassbinder himself) when he ends the film with a quotation from Thomas Mann: "I tell you that I am often sick to death of describing the human without participating in what is human." The quote comes from the fourth chapter of *Tonio Kröger*, near the end of the story, when the hero sits on the veranda contemplating the objects of his love through a glass door.

Thomas Mann has made the association between this feeling of isolation and his heroes' middleclass origins. In Fassbinder's films, also, we often get the impression that class affiliation is the real prison of his characters. Hints of this can be seen in Effi's behavior towards the servants, although she herself draws no conclusions from it. Effi Briest and Nora Helmer are tragic figures for precisely the reason that, given their level of consciousness, they are not in a position to understand the prisonlike quality of their lives. Fassbinder shows them behind lattices and curtains, as if they were ensnared in ornamentation. But they themselves seem not to notice these gilded cages, and even if they were in a position to do so, they would probably only observe how beautifully their cages were decorated. They can as little understand their circumscribed worlds as Martha can perceive hers as anything other than a kind of madhouse. These characters live in a double prison: not only do they experience their concrete social limitations as walls set up around them by conventions and rules, but these barriers separating them from the possibility for a better life exist in their minds as well. It could be said that the one type of prison is always a prerequisite for the other. When Effi Briest visits the apothecary we see a barred window behind her head and a veil over her face.

None of Fassbinder's protagonists succeed in smashing the glass wall which keeps them from an authentic life. And if one of them were to succeed, it would merely be to encounter another prison—like those wooden dolls which, opened, reveal another doll inside, which, in turn, contains still another doll. The hero of *Welt am Draht,* certainly, makes an incursion into the real world, but only after he has changed his identity. He will live as a guest among real people, but even so, only with the help of a woman who loves him because he reminds her of someone else: the doll in the doll in the doll. This multiplicity of prisons already characterizes *Love Is Colder than Death.* Its opening sequence takes place in a jail set up by a crime syndicate; in this criminal world, already isolated from normal life, we have another enclosure, like a cage in a cage. We might interpret the aquarium which decorates one of the rooms in *Welt am Draht* as a similar kind of symbolism.

Douglas Sirk

In *Imitation of Life,* one of Douglas Sirk's major works and a favorite film of Fassbinder's, the characters also live in prisons, separated from real life. In all their lives "nothing is natural. Never. Not in the whole film. And yet, each tries desperately to make their thoughts and their desires their own."[3] Each pursues a dream derived from the real world: the blacks from the white, the young from their elders, the poor from the rich, and even in their work, each is occupied with imitating someone else's life; it is not by accident that the main characters in the film are a photographer, an actress and a young woman who works as a singer and dancer. So, when we look at Lana Turner in *Imitation of Life,* we see on the screen the image of an actress playing an actress who plays characters thought up by a playwright who is played by an actor whom we can see on the screen. It is an almost total imitation which, however, represents real life, because "we are nearest to waking when when we dream that we are dreaming."[4] *Imitation of Life* is a key film for Fassbinder, not only because of the theme of inauthentic lives, but also as an example of the dramatic utilization of mirrors. Often a mirror mediates the action by framing an image in the image, so that the characters in such moments usually do the same thing we do: they look at themselves in the mirror image, so that we must almost believe that we see ourselves on the screen. The screen becomes a mirror.

Quotes

Fassbinder was already using the technique of infinite multiplication in his early films. For example, in *Love Is Colder than Death,* Ulli Lommel imitates Alain Delon in one of Jean-Pierre Melville's gangster films, while in turn, Melville had Delon act as if he were Humphrey Bogart playing Raymond Chandler's Philip Marlowe. We encounter this role-playing in Fassbinder's films not only in the realm of filmic quotations; it is also part of the essential behavior of his characters. In his early gangster films this game of masks was symbolized by the wearing of sunglasses. In later films the role-playing is often readable in the interpretation of details. When Marion and Jochen quarrel in the bar in the second part of *Eight Hours Are Not a Day* we see at the exit, as the two are leaving, the figure of a cherub and a Charles Bronson poster, symbols of the roles in which they saw themselves when they began their argument—he, a tough guy and she, a kind of angel. And because they saw themselves in these roles, we can surmise, they ended up fighting. The characters are imprisoned in their roles, and when Franz leaves the Munich-Stadelheim jail at the beginning of *Gods of the Plague,* only the illusion of freedom awaits him, because there can be no freedom in a world which is experienced by its inhabitants as a prison.

In *Die Niklashauser Fahrt* finally, the nostalgia for cinematic prototypes becomes identical with the conjuring up of key political images, since not only historical reality is quoted in this film, but also Glauber Rocha's *Antonio das Mortes,* which is itself the conjuring up of a legendary figure, so that what we see is actually the quotation of a quotation. When we realize that Rocha's film was never able to serve the political function for which it was intended in Brazil because of the prevailing political climate at the time it was made, then *Niklashauser Fahrt,* this German film about the failure of a political protest movement, becomes a utopian representation of a utopian representation. The doll-in-the-doll approach, with its perspective directed, it might be said, towards infinity, is therefore not an expression of hopelessness, but precisely the yearning, the hope (for utopia): it is the form which corresponds most closely to utopian thinking.

Barriers to Language

Fassbinder's people are even imprisoned by their speech, which binds them to a totally determined environment. When Jorgos, the Greek immigrant worker in *Katzelmacher,* mumbles his "Alle ich Bumbum... Ich nix verstehn,"[5] it is as if someone had pushed him up against a wall which will isolate him from any possible communication with his fellow human beings. Yet, language hardly serves Fassbinder's other characters any more effectively as a means of communication. Ironically, language is the perfect medium for informers and liars. Denunciation plays a role in a large number of Fassbinder's films, and everyone seems capable of becoming an informer; friends, colleagues, lovers. Almost all Fassbinder's characters lie. In the opening scenes of many films we witness such lies: Petra von Kant lies to her mother over the telephone, as does Hanna in *Rios das Mortes,* and Martha lies in a similar sequence to her father.

In Fassbinder's view, language is above all a tool in the service of the ruling class, an additional means through which they take the world into possession. The executives and foremen in *Eight Hours Are Not a Day* speak a kind of master-language, as does Fabian's father in *Pioneers in Ingolstadt* when he gives orders to his son, or Harald in *Eight Hours* when he takes his wife to task. It is not by chance that he speaks to her this way, because, as Grandma explains in the fourth part of the series, "They really don't go together... she's just a worker's daughter and he wears a tuxedo." Harald's language only provides further evidence of the social distance between himself and his wife. Conversely, Kurt Raab's wife in *Why Does Herr R Run Amok?* comes from a higher social class than he, and the fact that language

Love Is Colder than Death

serves her and her ilk better than it does him renders him
speechless, and is finally the release mechanism which drives
him to murder. Many people in Fassbinder's films take
refuge in silence. The exploited Marlene in *Petra von Kant*
goes through life without speaking. Others manage to become silent, like Hans in *Merchant of the Four Seasons.*
"You can't really talk," Marie tells Jorgos in *Katzelmacher,*
"and that's what I like best." In *Beware of a Holy Whore,*
Eddie, who has barely mastered the German language, is certainly the closest of all the characters to genuine life.

Other characters express themselves vaguely, almost always ending their sentences with a superfluous "...or whatever," "...or so," "...and so," or "after all." Or they use
such abbreviated forms of acknowledgement that their
speech almost never conveys more than an expression of feeling: this is especially true of exclamations like "crazy,"
"logical" and "exactly," which we hear repeatedly in Fassbinder's films. There are many scenes in which we witness
how people who are rendered speechless by circumstance
often use the telephone, which is so obviously a substitute for

more direct communication, as a means to avoid any real understanding. In many other scenes we experience the degeneration of the beginnings of conversation into stammering as, in general, in each film several levels of grammatical possibility are present. They extend from silence to the stringing together of conditioned responses, so that a language of communication almost never develops. Still, these levels of expression have the important function of allowing us to experience language in a social hierarchy: amid the linguistic poverty of *Katzelmacher,* we have the Greek immigrant worker, a subproletarian played by an intellectual. The virtual inability of the oppressed to express themselves serves only to intensify their oppression. It also becomes apparent that relationships within groups are reflected in language: as they sit around the table, Fassbinder's characters talk in a manner that seems more directed to us than to one another. And if their language begins to make sense, it is often only because they aspire "to climb the social ladder, to speak the 'refined,' 'elevated' German of the upper classes."[6]

From time to time, when someone in these films dares to call a thing by its real name, the moment of truth makes its appearance amid all the phony talk as it does when children speak out in fairy tales or when fools and clowns have their say in Shakespeare. In the third part of *Eight Hours,* a worker interrupts the foreman to ask him about a word in the latter's pep talk he didn't understand—"What's that? A maxim?" In the second part of the same series, Grandma bursts out laughing at a form she reads at the police station, and remarks to the miffed officials, "Your way of talking is funny, isn't it?" Those who are not ultimately as oppressed by language defend themselves in some instances with its help —they fight back with words. We see this in the sequence in *Fear Eats the Soul* in which Emmi sits with Ali in an outdoor cafe and shouts to the onlookers, "Stop gaping, you stupid pigs! This is my husband! My husband!", or when, in the second part of *Eight Hours,* Grandma introduces Gregor as her "beloved." In such moments, nothing more happens than that someone has dared to call a thing by its real name.

In the love scenes, hardly a word is spoken, and if there is, it is usually a regression to the language of childhood. "I'm from Munich, got a girlfriend there. I like her a whole lot," says Franz in *Love Is Colder than Death*. In *Welt am Draht*, Margit Carstensen talks almost like a child when she says, "You, I love you even now." While she utters this sentence, we see a doll on her bed, as in other instances in Fassbinder's films where the bedrooms of girls and women are decorated with dolls and statues of cherubs. But what is still sayable in the language of children is no longer possible in the world of adults. Here, everything is corrupted, although we can, if need be, surmise the truth when language breaks through the appearance of untruthfulness. In the final sequence of *Jail Bait*, when Hanni says during the murder trial, "The truth is, it wasn't real love, it was just physical with us," we see something that Hanni doesn't—Franz's face—and when he tells Hanni, "I agree, we were never really in love," we see just the opposite in his face.

The love scenes between Hanna Schygulla and Harry Baer in *Pioneers in Ingolstadt* are perhaps the most beautiful in German cinema since Murnau. In these dialogues the woman sees something in the face of the man that we are also allowed to see because the camera shows it to us, and this is the humaneness of which this man is capable, but which he long ago lost the courage to show, having learned that one gets along better in this world by being tough, and so, hides his humanity behind a brutal way of speaking. In the midst of this deceitful chatter, through the silent image, something better is discernible.

Utopia

What seems to be love can end in treachery *(Love Is Colder than Death)* or in total repression *(Martha)*. Eva's love for Stiller in *Welt am Draht* only grants him a kind of borrowed existence. Even the heroic alliance between Emmi and Ali can never again be as harmonious as it was in the beginning. Everyone fails in love, and must fail, because "There is no right living in a wrong life."[7]

At the end of *American Soldier*, when Ricky's brother

throws himself on his corpse, the sequence takes on the quality of a ceremony through the use of the slow-motion camera. An instant becomes like an eternity to our subjective sense of time. This effect is also obtained in the closing scene in *Welt am Draht,* where the camera cranes back and forth intermittently, and cross cutting is used in such a way that our sense of the passage of time is brought to a halt. But such moments of eternity are only promises, like the first meeting of Margit Carstensen and Karlheinz Bohm in *Martha.* Reality does not bear out these promises, and love remains a utopia. Perhaps because of this, love is more important to Fassbinder than to any other contemporary German director. As he puts it, There's actually no love, there's only the possibility of love.''

Fassbinder's characters all have, as he has said himself, ''something like a hope, and that is the yearning for a utopia.'' Often these utopias have a location—Greece or some other southern European country (*Katzelmacher* and *Gods of the Plague),* or South America *(Rio das Mortes).* But what the characters have is actually more a desire than any concrete idea about their utopias; the hero in *Rio das Mortes* thinks the Mayans lived in Peru, not Mexico. In an inverted world, utopia becomes somewhat shabby as soon as it must make its appearance in reality. In *Katzelmacher,* Helga, who has saved her money so diligently to become an actress, can only, in the long run, become disillusioned. In the same film, Marie's dreamed-of trip to Greece, if it ever came to pass, would only end in catastrophe, since the Greek is from all accounts already married with two children. The trip to Chicago which should have improved Hanna's prospects for a decent life in *Whity,* in the end seems so horrible to her and Whity that they prefer suicide. In such instances it becomes apparent that even utopia turns out to be flawed. Utopia will often be experienced by Fassbinder's people only as a caricature. The leather jackets of the young men in *Katzelmacher* with ''Chicago Rockers'' emblazoned on them offer the same caracature as the jacket with the word ''Korea'' on it that Franz wears in *Jail Bait,* a film which was originally to be titled *Korean Spring.*[8] In *Merchant of the Four Seasons,* the former Foreign Legionnaire, with shining eyes, asks his old buddy, ''Remember Morocco in '47?'' Effi Briest refers to "the time when I was sick, which was really almost the most beautiful time of my life," and in *Katzelmacher* Marie confesses, "I love you too, I know it, because it hurts so much." These are all declarations in which the inverted world raises its voice: the most terrifying things—war, sickness, pain—assume the highest value.

When utopia is not removed from the contradictions of the times, why shouldn't it be sought after even in the promise of happiness offered by mass-produced oil paintings, in which the utopian *promesse de bonheur* becomes as overaccentuated as the sex characteristics of a pin-up photo. Almost all of Fassbinder's characters decorate the rooms in which they live with pictures; with posters of pop singers and riders into the sunset, with paintings of Alpine landscapes and ocean vistas. In higher social circles, utopia will be pursued at another level. Petra von Kant has a reproduction of a Poussin on her wall (and at one point, she lies beside it in the same pose as one of the sleeping forms in the painting). In *Jail Bait*, in the scene in which the mother waits for the father (who in the meantime has been shot), we see her head foregrounded against a picture of an Alpine lake and island. It opens up behind the woman's head and directs our gaze into a depth which her face alone cannot express, but which corresponds to her psychological state. So these rooms, adorned with reproductions, must "not in any case correspond to a realistic environment in which these characters might actually live, but more to their inner psyches; these are rooms which are potentially more than rooms, inhabited by the minds of the characters." (Fassbinder) How miserable a world can look in which even these mutilated utopias are found wanting, is evident in *Why Does Herr R Run Amok?* But what counts for Fassbinder, as he says about *Martha,* is that even a film of this kind contains "something positive, since naturally everyone who sees it wants to be contrasted to it, and this must quite simply make it something else." Therefore, Herr R is not a film about, but a polemic against the banality of modern life. It shows us middle-class people in about the same light as Bunuel presents Catholic priests. Occasionally, these symbolic backdrops are missing in Fassbinder: in *Merchant of the Four Seasons* when Hans drinks himself to death, we see a bare wall behind his head. Life without utopia is death.

In the latter film the utopia of the man who drinks himself to death has already been literally shattered: he has smashed a phonograph record of the popular song "Buona Buona Notte," which had been the expression of his dreams. Thought can never assume the function of utopia for Fassbinder's characters. "We never think too much, but more likely too little," Hans is advised by his sister at one point. "Really?" he answers, "But that's torture for me." In *Welt am Draht* almost everyone dies who dares to formulate the idea that their lives might not be authentic, but only simulated. It is not thought, but dreaming that enriches life. Fassbinder says, "As far as I go when I think, I find no hope. It is only past that point, when I can let my thoughts run away with me, that I see any." To arouse that hope is the duty of art.

Imagination

The workers on *Eight Hours Are Not a Day* have a desire for utopia, but no clear notion of it. At the close of each segment we see a red sun over the smoking factory chimneys. Soot gushes out of the smokestacks and the sun climbs quickly up into the sky with the help of a fast-motion camera. The shot achieves a pictorial rhythm which does not so much correspond with the characters as it offers an interpretation of them to the audience. It becomes apparent that these workers, who can no longer see their utopia, are in a state of alienation which "no longer involves only the individual self-alienation of individual workers, but rather, has grown into the collective self-alienation of a whole class, to the detriment of their consciousness of their own position in the social structure."[9] So the series certainly does not lack a perspective; it is just that this perspective is measured in terms of alienation. Fassbinder says, "I believe that the workers, by first making changes within the system (when they succeed), become sensitized for a different and perhaps more human system." Only through meaningful change will the notion of a better future become conceivable, and only through the notion of a better future will meaningful change become possible. "We're so hung up on the way things are," complains a worker in the fifth part of *Eight Hours,* "that we just can't imagine anything different any more." In *Niklashauser Fahrt* there is no improvement in existing circumstances, because the people cannot imagine a better situation as anything concrete. Utopia is perhaps a dead issue with them, but they are actually still part of an ongoing process involving ongoing work. "Do you believe it's worth the trouble, always struggling and struggling?" demands the wife of the worker Franz in the third part of *Eight Hours;* "If we win, you bet!" he answers. In this television series, Fassbinder has given us an example of how art can participate in the process of enlightenment. Many of his more recent films stand on their own merits, even if we measure them by the criteria of social theory alone; for example, *Fear Eats the Soul,* in which, among other things, discrimination against foreign workers' psychosomatic illness and the emotional deterioration of the older generation, are dealt with in the context of a feature film.

Victims of Education

In Fassbinder's films, the oppressed are victims. He leaves no doubt that false relations spring from other false relations. "Have you come back from the war healthy?" the mother in *American Soldier* asks her son, who has just returned from Vietnam. "I'm OK, Mom," he answers laconically. "And we," shouts the father in *Jail Bait,* "we weren't kids, we were soldiers!" In *Pioneers in Ingolstadt* a soldier declares nonchalantly, "Where there isn't a war, you have to make one." The degrading working conditions to which the young man in *Jail Bait* is exposed are made evident in the brief but extremely graphic sequences in the poultry slaughterhouse. In order to portray the father in this film as a victim, Fassbinder originally intended to include "a scene showing the father at work," in order to demonstrate "as clearly as possible the oppression with which he is faced on the job, but which he

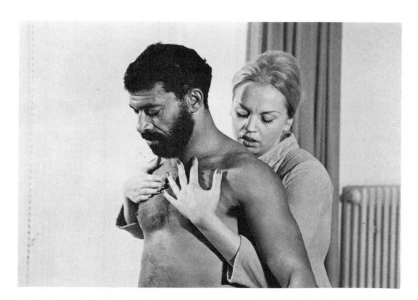

Fear Eats the Soul

then, in turn, unfortunately only passes on—and that should not be allowed.''[10] Education functions as the perfect instrument of oppression. Adults like the title character in *Martha* and Hans in *Merchant of the Four Seasons* are victims of this process of conditioning; in *Effi Briest* and *Nora Helmer* grown men attempt to educate their adult wives, and in *Jail Bait,* we can see how each generation uses the next as a kind of educational garbage dump. When Hanni imagines, as a sadistic joke, how her boyfriend might be castrated, she speaks precisely like the daughter of a father who would consider castration a fit punishment for Franz. "Children don't need to be happy, Monika," declares the austere Harald in the fourth part of *Eight Hours Are Not a Day,* "Children must be prepared for life."

Reifications

In this life for which children must be prepared, human relations are for the most part similar to relations to things.

Marlene in *Petra von Kant* is treated like an object; in *Nora Helmer* emotional ties are identical with property relations; Ali, in *Fear Eats the Soul*, is made into a sexual object when Barbara Valentin undresses him, and again, when the good-natured Emmi shows off his muscles to her friends. Often relations with things are more loving than those with other people. Martha is more upset by the loss of her handbag than by the death of her father. The men in *Gods of the Plague* lovingly caress a Mercedes in the barnyard, and only with difficulty can the young man in *Rio das Mortes* leave his car with the auto dealer—first he wants to hear that the vehicle will be well taken care of. The same is true of the man who sells Hans the fruit cart in *Merchant of the Four Seasons.*

"You know," someone says in *Holy Whore,* "society has made him into something so dead, he can't react from within any more." In Fassbinder's films we can often see how people are deprived of the ability to act intuitively. For example, in the first part of *Eight Hours,* when Jochen hangs up the telephone after one call, he decides to dial another number. He already has his finger on the dial when he notices something and hangs up; he has forgotten that he is using a public phone, which costs money, and he doesn't have the correct change. In *Katzelmacher* and *Jail Bait* (in which the father explains that "without money, there's no love..."), love is determined by financial considerations—not always, certainly, but reified relationships are still the norm. When Whity visits Hanna, he tells her cautiously, "I can pay, if you want," though it is obvious that this is not what she wants. But where did Whity get this idea? Money is a means of exchange to which he has grown accustomed, because it possesses a validity that crosses the barriers of color; tenderness, which would have been more appropriate, does not. In the last scene of *Jail Bait,* an immigrant worker who was once a friend of the accused youth passes him by without a greeting and disappears behind a door upon which, as we see in closeup, the word "Cash" is written. He has become part of the existing order.

Such behavior is comprehensible in principle in Fassbinder's films because it isn't the characters, but rather, their material needs, which make them act so inhumanely. "There's lots of enlightenment and lots of freedom out there," sneers the father in *Jail Bait,* "for anyone who can pay lots of money." With this statement he is giving the reason for his own anti-enlightenment attitudes, even if he seems to believe what he says only cynically. This detailing of the characters is characteristic of Fassbinder. In *Eight Hours,* for instance, he maintains that "if there had been further chapters in the series, the motivations of all the characters would have become clearer and more evident." There should have been, and would have to have been, actually, a chapter for each character, where the specific background of each could be explored—why and what in the social structure and the family made them the way they are—what produced their possibilities and impossibilities." Then, it would be obvious what motivates the worker Jurgen to feel so little solidarity with the other workers, and we might be able to understand how Miss Erlkonig was able to conquer her prejudices, as we see in the last part of the series, by falling in love with a worker.

This kind of meaningful insight into each character very possibly requires a staging which deliberately avoids realistic detail. In a Fassbinder film, when a popular song is heard, it is usually just a bit out-of-date, and even the paintings are more old-fashioned than they would be in reality; where the real-life counterpart of the film character might long since have had a reproduction of Van Gogh's "Sunflowers" on the wall. When the workers in *Eight Hours* go out drinking, they are a little too well-dressed, and even the tavern looks much too bourgeois. This deliberately incorrect staging hinders precisely our ability to make easy connections. Because we no longer judge the pictures on the wall in relation to our own, but stop to think about them, the whole scene becomes a paradigm, and we make comparisons, instead of simply reacting emotionally. Fassbinder carries this principle into the synchronization of sound by dubbing voices: for example, Kurt Raab's voice in *Merchant of the Four Seasons* "was

dubbed by Peter Gauhe, who has a very average voice, of the
type that this character had to have, and which makes him
somehow more human. I did the same thing with Irm Hermann in *Effi Briest,* by dubbing in Margit Carstensen's
voice."

Everything Changes

Fassbinder's people change. In the fourth part of *Eight
Hours Are Not a Day,* when Marion wants to convince
Jochen that Miss Erlkonig would be a suitable member of
their wedding party, she says that her friend has a "good
heart," to which he answers, "You're the only one who sees
it." She adds, as an afterthought, "Well, all the same..."
—which is not supposed to mean that she is just imagining
something that isn't true at all, but that she recognizes in
Miss Erlkonig an objectively established possibility. In the
third part of the series, Grandma puts forth her own dialectical method when she counters Gregor's remark "Things
just are the way they are," with an emphatic "That's exactly
what they're not." Words and sentences can change meaning
when the context changes, and people's behavior changes
when their interests have changed. This is noticeable time and
again as early as *Katzelmacher,* and is especially marked in
Fear Eats the Soul in the changing attitudes of Emmi's family, friends and neighbors toward her marriage. This can go to
grotesque lengths, as when in *Eight Hours* the employer, of
all people, must inform the workers about their differing interests, or in *Katzelmacher,* when Elisabeth, who has taken
the greatest advantage of the Greek, tells her colleagues that
he shouldn't be called a "foreign worker" but a "guest
worker." When Emmi in *Fear Eats the Soul* declares that her
first husband was a "foreign worker from Poland," the objective point of the story becomes obvious: her humanity was
concealed in her inhumanity, and now ventures timidly away
from it. Emmi's attitudes are already more humanely developed than her speech. Her decency, when it finally comes to
light, is stuck in the form of the Nazi word "Fremdarbeiter"
as, so to speak, the eggshells of barbarism still stick to the

feathers of human development. In Fassbinder's films, the exterior look of a specific historical period may be accurately reconstructed, like the Adenauer era in *Merchant of the Four Seasons,* but this accuracy of detail is not necessary to demonstrate the power of human beings to decisively influence history in the real world.[11] Fassbinder doesn't show fascism, but he does show how fascistic behavior originates.

Sickness and Death

Under intense social pressure, what is generally called "human nature" may undergo unexpected changes. For this reason, in Fassbinder's films illnesses are psychosomatic, like Hans' first collapse in *Merchant* or Ali's stress-induced gastric ulcer in *Fear Eats the Soul.* Death appears as a kind of passive answer to social conflict (the foreman in the first part of *Eight Hours).* Even those deaths which occur as if a command had been issued by the subconscious have social causes, as when Hans drinks himself to death in *Merchant.* In the art of earlier centuries, death was usually presented as a punishment for "sins," and this theological conception has survived in secular form in the novels of the nineteenth century and to this day in Hollywood films. In this instance, even if the immediate cause of death is a bullet, it nevertheless only hits the person who, according to the ground rules of all-knowing dramatic tradition, must make his exit, so that in the end, who has sinned least survives. Now that there is no God to command life and death, the commands come from the subconscious of the characters—a psychological interpretation of death. Where Fassbinder's approach departs from this interpretation is perhaps most obvious if we compare his science fiction film *Welt am Draht* with any other "computer" film or novel (including the one on which the film is based). While in traditional sci-fi stories, it is usually suggested that people may be the powerless servants of an all-powerful authority, Fassbinder leaves no doubt that whoever made this false world so false has an interest in keeping it that way; these are definite people with very definite interests. Neither the theologian nor the psychoanalyst is capable any longer of diagnosing the cause of death in this world. Of all directors, only Fassbinder, as far as I can see, has understood the human body as an arena of social conflict.

Homeless Heroes

Fassbinder is himself an arena of history, in the double sense that the word implies (in German, the word Geschichte means "history" and "story" or "narrative"—RM); he narrates the story of an individual life, which in turn reflects a period of political history. Indeed, Fassbinder encodes more self-references into his films and develops aspects of his private life more skilfully than any other contemporary German director. His personal life, as it is reflected in the preferences and aversions we see in his films, has a very direct bearing on concrete political history, because these films also have to do with things like how a revolution fails, how people attempt to work in an anti-authoritarian life situation, how they struggle against conventions and gradually learn solidarity...

If we could condense all Fassbinder's heroes into a single film character, we would get at least the outlines of a mythic figure who might best be described as a fatherless young person who, continually in flight from a terrible past, believes he can realize his dreams, though they are still far away from him. This is a person who feels like a stranger in his own country. The immigrant workers in Fassbinder's films —strangers in a strange land—are a kind of inverted image of their young German counterparts. These are people with a wanderlust which is at bottom equivalent to homesickness, because they always seem to be searching for their national identity—a theme that has already played a central role in German Romanticism, where we find the figure of the German with a yearning for southern lands, a kindred soul to the Mignon figures associated in German lore with wandering orphans and gypsy children. This is a national myth, like the gun-toting loner in American fiction. Alexander Kluge's *Yesterday Girl (Abscheid von Gestern)* and perhaps even

Fear Eats the Soul

Volker Schlondorff's *Mord und Totschlag* are other examples of this tendency. It is to Fassbinder's credit that in all of New German Cinema, these two films have the most in common with his work. To be sure, only Fassbinder has continually stressed this theme, and just as this motif has undergone transformations in the German art of the last two hundred years, so it has been altered even further in Fassbinder's films as a mirror image of political history.

Of all the events in recent German history, the most significant for Fassbinder's generation was the rise of a politicized youth movement in the late sixties, and its failure, which was foreshadowed by the May events in Paris in 1968. Fassbinder's films, with the exception of the three shorts, grew out of this critical period. They all reflect that sense of melancholy which inevitably makes its appearance as a leitmotiv in European art following the defeat of a revolution. The feeling of living in a totally distorted society which has denied its own best possibilities, and in which the majority of the citizens don't even know what has happened, does not figure in Fassbinder's "world." It is more consistent with the

Fox and His Friends

feelings of his contemporaries, or at least those of his contemporaries from the educated middle class—that layer of society which, in Western countries, is the usual breeding-ground for artists.

The Labor Process of Truth

Fassbinder's films are post-revolutionary films, and in a very specific sense, "post-revolutionary" means utopian. This is a kind of utopian thinking which no longer steers a course for the naive pre-revolutionary dream of a better world, but which has absorbed the fragments of a negative historical experience. This utopia is not anywhere outside our world, but lies deep within it, like the doll in the doll. Therefore, the dramaturgy in Fassbinder's films maintains a perspective throughout which continually opens up new vistas for us, and yet, in the vanishing point, shows us only ourselves.

Even Fassbinder's turn toward the cliches of the culture industry is related to this negative political experience, which is dealt with in *Niklashauser Fahrt.* For if a political movement fails, does this not suggest certain consequences for aesthetics? For example, along with political failure, a certain kind of politically oriented art, which previously had been involved in explaining events and making preparations, also fails. Godard's film practice, which sought to anticipate political developments symbolically through the revolutionizing of the narrative, could only be considered revolutionary up until May, 1968. The fact that Fassbinder has been attempting since *Merchant of the Four Seasons* to create a new popular art is related to his political experience, because after an aborted revolution, society no longer offers the same conditions for class struggle as before. (Most of the semi-documentary "workplace" films which today are considered to be models of politically enlightened art, could be reproached on the grounds that they seem not to have taken notice of this change.)

In his book "Die Angestellten," Siegfried Kracauer has analyzed this confused social situation, in which a largely bourgeoisified working class has existed in Germany since 1918. Odon von Horvath wrote in 1932 that Germany had "like all remaining European nations, up to ninety percent (of its population) from the actual or would-be petty bourgeoisie, in any case then, from the petty bourgeoisie. If I wish to give an account of the masses from this information, I may naturally hesitate to describe only ten percent..."[12] Besides Horvath, writers like Marieluise Fleisser and Hans Fallada also attempted at the time to reach precisely this large audience with a new popular art which would portray them with understanding and address them critically. A similar situation has existed since May, 1968. Fassbinder's popular art is an attempt to respond artistically to this situation. The contradictory nature of the masses, which he demonstrates in his plays and films, is mirrored in their language, as in their plots and action. This was as important for Marieluise Fleisser as it is for Fassbinder. For both, false consciousness signifies alienation.

Consequently, Fassbinder is concerned with the false consciousness of his audience. Because the true does not exist outside the false, just as art is not to be found beyond kitsch.

Art is the exception, while kitsch, which is the expression of false consciousness in a false world, is the norm. Kitsch is not the perversion of art, but art the triumph over kitsch. In this sense, art lies hidden in trash, as the truth is in lies. The important thing is to force it out. Truth is work.

This is why Fassbinder is so productive.

Footnotes

1. *Filmkritik,* Aug. 1969, p. 472.
2. Unless otherwise indicated, all Fassbinder's remarks in this article come from an interview conducted on February 20, 1974 in Berlin.
3. Fassbinder in *Fernsehen und Film,* Feb. 1971, p. 12.
4. Novalis, Postscript to *Blutenstaub,* N. 15.
5. The quotations from *Katzelmacher* are taken from the script for the theatrical production (R. W. Fassbinder, Antiteater, 3rd Ed., Frankfurt 1973, pp. 7-30, Edition Suhrkamp Vol. 443). My quotations may not agree word for word with the text of the film. The film has also amplified the contents of the play somewhat. "The film begins much earlier than the play, which starts when the Greek comes in. The film shows what the relationships between the people in the group were before the Greek broke in on them. There are other differences, but that's the main one." (Fassbinder, see above.) A few other minor details were changed: the girl who hopes to be an actress in the film dreams of a future as a pop singer in the play.
6. Walter Benjamin; 1929, in his *Critique of the Fiction of Marieluise Fleisser,* quoted in G. Ruhle (Ed.), *Materialien zum Leben und Schreiben der Marieluise Fleisser,* Frankfurt 1973, p. 141 (Edition Suhrkamp Vol. 594).
7. Theodor W. Adorno, *Minima Moralia,* N. 18.
8. Fassbinder: "I originally wanted to call the film *Korean Spring* because of that jacket, which had the word on it, and because for me, Korea had to do with war...but this they (the production company and the broadcasting network of Free Berlin) would not tolerate, unfortunately." (see above.)
9. Werner Hoffman, Pauperization, in E. Th. Mohl (Ed.), *Folgen einer Theorie, Essays uber "Das Kapital" von Karl Marx,* 3rd Ed., Frankfurt, 1969, p. 60 (Edition Suhrkamp Vol. 226).

10. Fassbinder has explained the most significant difference between his film and the Franz Xaver Kroetz play: "In my opinion the boy was the real victim, and not both kids. That is the difference, the essential point. The boy is the victim and the three others, the father, the mother and the girl, are as far as I'm concerned products of the establishment, while the boy is (in the film) the outsider—not the young couple, only the young man." (See above.)

11. The reason why the uniforms in *Pioneers in Ingolstadt* appear to bear signs of Hitlerism (at one point, we see a swastika on Harry Baer's cap) is explained by Fassbinder: "I wanted to make the film with Bundeswehr uniforms, because I thought it would be the safest, least conspicuous thing to do. If I worked with swastikas or whatever, I thought the costumes would be too obtrusive, whereas if we used Bundeswehr uniforms, it would be more subtle. This seemed like an act of aggression to the ZDF (Zweite Deutsches Fernsehen, the television network), so they prohibited it, and we had to begin again with the old German uniforms and Hitler uniforms...We didn't bother about the costumes any more. We just got hold of some old costumes, we didn't care if they were French or English or whatever." (See above.) In this way, Fassbinder evoked a certain element of timelessness in this Fleisser play, which was actually written in the 1920s. For a director of Fassbinder's skill, it would have been easy to re-create the outward look of the Hitler era. In the barracks square, a wall was visible not far away with the symbol of the antiatomic weapons movement. The symbol "was not painted on especially," but "it was there, and so I decided to leave it." (See above.) The fact that he let it stay, although he could just as easily have gotten rid of it, is characteristic not only of Fassbinder's style (which always gives prominence to trivial details) but seems also to relate to his way of depicting history, which is most evident in *Niklashauser Fahrt*. In that film, he used sets from several historical epochs, in order to create a well-defined consciousness of the historical process which continues to this day.

Interview with Rainer Werner Fassbinder

By Wilfried Wiegand

In your early life, were there any decisive cultural or religious influences on you from your family, school, church?

What's essential is that I grew up in a semi-chaotic household, a household that didn't conform to bourgeois norms.

But wasn't it actually a bourgeois milieu? Wasn't your father a doctor and your mother a translator?

Well, all right, because everyone has to make a living. But it was a house where the rules and regulations that normally exist in families didn't hold. I actually grew up almost without parents. I lived virtually alone very early in life, for example, from the ages of seven to nine quite alone, though there were people in the house because my mother, who was sick, rented out rooms, but there wasn't anyone who looked after me or that sort of thing. And then in this house, in this dwelling, as I remember there was nothing but literature and art. When they gave me a gift, they gave me a volume of Durer, when I was five...

Five?

Oh yes. And when my father came to visit, I don't know, every five years or so, he'd come passing through and read Faust with me on a tape and things like that.

Were your parents divorced?

They got divorced in 1951, when I was five. But even before that, when they were still together, nobody ever told me, "This is how you do it" or "You're not allowed to do that," and so forth. I really grew up like a little flower.

Your mother often appears in your films. Is she an actress?

She is now.

Your heroes are usually fatherless. Is this autobiographical?

That would certainly be the case, because everything I do and that interests me in the long run somehow or other has to do with me. It also occurs to me, however, that there are always brothers in my films...

Do you have any of your own?

Not a one.

Would you have liked to have had one?

Certainly, I probably would have liked having one, what they call a brother, someone who would have offered a possibility of contact that I otherwise wouldn't have.

You don't have any sisters, either?

No, none.

What about religious influences? Crucifixes and pictures of the madonna have played a large role in your films ever since you began using set designs; even in the science fiction world of Welt am Draht *there's a crucifix on the wall.*

That has more to do with my friends than with me.

With anyone in particular?

With Peer Raben and Kurt Raab. Peer Raben was the person I worked with most often when I began to do films and theatre, and he was something of an influence on me. He had a very unusual relationship to religion, which I got to understand, and may have absorbed, in a way, because I myself have had almost no experience with religion.

What sort of experience did he have? Did he feel oppressed?

I don't know, it was a very strange relationship, perhaps even an oppressive one...

But in any case, he was stamped by religion.

Stamped, yes. And Kurt Raab...

Who does the sets?

Yes, he still does them.

Negatively influenced by Catholicism?

Yes. But how Catholicism affected them never seemed a concrete problem for me, but just something, as I understood it, that can play an influential role in people's lives.

Then the scene in Why Does Herr R Run Amok? *when the two old school friends (played by Kurt Raab and Peer Raben) talk about their childhood and singing in the choir, is authentic?*

It's a totally authentic scene. Those two have known each other for a long time. They went to school in Straubing together.

By the way, even when you don't design the sets, don't they have to be approved by you?

That is supervised by me, too. It's not true that Kurt Raab furnishes sets unless we've talked about it and worked out in advance what the end result should be.

You began using set designs in Gods of the Plague.

With *Gods of the Plague,* yes.

Didn't you leave school shortly before graduation to go to drama school?

First I went to my father in Cologne. I lived there three years, and managed an office, a real estate office, and worked for a decorator in the evenings, so I can paper walls and paint like a professional, and so can always make a living doing that. I worked on rooms that had been reconstructed into smaller compartments and rented to immigrant workers.

Is that one of the reasons why you're interested in the subject?

At that time I came to understand the problems of the immigrant workers and developed a definite affinity to them.

How did you meet the Action Theater people?

They were together at the same drama school, and I simply came there; they all knew one another, were already a group, which I joined.

I read somewhere that you also worked in the archives of the Suddeutsche Zeitung.

Yes. I worked there for two years while I was in drama school.

You have no training as a film director?

Well, I took the entrance examination, which I didn't pass.

Where?

Berlin.

At the Berlin Film and Television Academy? When, then?

1965.

No, really?

Yes. Naturally, I wasn't the only one. Werner Schroeter didn't pass either, and neither did Rosa (von Praunheim).

Is that really true? Then it hasn't changed much since the nineteenth century, when the really good painters were active outside the academies. So then you went from theatre to film...

I didn't go from theatre to film, I went from film to theatre. I made two short films *(Der Stadtstreicher* and *Die Kleine Chaos)* in 1965 and 1966, long before anti-teater.

So you did theatre then because film was simply too expensive and not going well?

Well, Christoph Roser produced those two short films for, I don't know, 15,000 or 18,000 DM, more or less, but at that time it was a great deal because we didn't have any money, or rather, I didn't have any money. So after I broke with Christoph Roser, I signed a promissory note for 18,000 DM, which I had to pay back at 300 DM a month, and at that point, everyone was starting to make films, but I didn't see any opportunity to do it myself.

Godard must have been a model for you in those days— Breathless *and* Band of Outsiders?

No, not those two. Since *Band of Outsiders* Godard doesn't interest me any more. There is one film by Godard that I've seen twenty-seven times, and that's *My Life to Live,* which is, together with Bunuel's *Viridiana* the most important film I've seen in my life.

But at the end of Love Is Colder than Death, *when Franz calls Joanna a whore, isn't that like the end of* Breathless?

Well, okay. But that was something I didn't do deliberately when I did it.

How about the influence of Melville on your early films, the gangster films? With you, and Melville as well, the brutality of the environment and of the police plays a smaller role than in Hollywood films. You and Melville are more concerned with a code of honor, with the relationship of friends to one another, and consequently, more with the subjective side of things.

But doesn't that really have to do with the fact that when we, as Europeans, do something that is derived from the American film experience, it is filtered through a European consciousness, and always results in something different? I don't think I really needed Melville as a model. *Der Stadt-streicher* has a great deal to do with Eric Rohmer's *Le Signe de Lion,* which was also a very important film for me.

When did you start going to the movies?

I've been seeing films since I was five, first, covered-wagon Westerns, and then, from the age of seven, I saw everything. I actually went to the movies every day, and later, two or three times a day, if possible.

And now?

I very seldom go to see films any more. I avoid it when I can and almost never see films about which a lot has been written.

Have there been any American films other than Sirk's that have substantially influenced you?

Yes, Raoul Walsh...

Which films, for instance?

Band of Angels, White Heat... The relationship between James Cagney and his mother is, I think, like that between all my heroes and their mothers. Then, Huston's *Asphalt Jungle* was very important, and Howard Hawks, the gay stories...

Which gay stories?

In Hawks, most of them.

You once wanted to write an article about Josef von Sternberg. What fascinated you about him?

What Sternberg does with light. The ability to tell stories indirectly, in a roundabout way. It's this extreme artificiality which is still, in my opinion, something very much alive.

That kind of artificiality plays a big part in your films, too.

I have always thought that the more beautiful, and well made, and better produced and edited films are, the freer and more liberating they are.

Are there any films in the New German Cinema that you especially admire?

Mord und Totschlag (Volker Schlondorff) and *48 Hours to Acapulco* (Klaus Lemke).

Has Straub influenced you?

Straub has been more like an important figure for me.

But weren't you inspired by him to use a slow narrative rhythm, and a principle of real time in which occurrences on the screen last exactly as long as they do in reality?

What was more significant for me was that Straub directed a play, *Krankheit der Jugend* (Ferdinand Bruckner) with the Action Theater, and even though his version was only ten minutes long, we rehearsed it for all of four months, over and over again, for only two hours a day, I admit, was it was still really crazy. This experience I had with Straub, who approached his work and the other people with such an air of comic solemnity, fascinated me. He would let us play a scene and then would say to us, "How did they feel at this point?"

The Bitter Tears of Petra Von Kant

This was really quite right in this case, because we ourselves had to develop an attitude about what we were doing, so that when we were acting, we developed the technique of looking at ourselves, and the result was that there was a distance between the role and the actor, instead of total identity. The films he's made that I think are very beautiful are the early ones, *Machorka Muff* and *Not Reconciled,* up to and including *Chronicle of Anna Magdalena Bach,* though *Othon* and other films since then have proved to me that what is most important to him is not what interests me in his work.

The anti-teater was in any case a sort of commune, and you once said about your early films that everyone concerned with them was basically an author. At that time, did you believe that works of art could be created in an anti-authoritarian way?

I thought that if I said it often enough, it would come true.

And that turned out to be an illusion?

Beware of a Holy Whore

It became apparent that exactly the opposite is true. Actually, it was already obvious to me in *Holy Whore* that I had worked for five years under an illusion which was utopian, but utopia made us sick. It was a beautiful dream, which we talked about time and again in the hope that it would come true. The news, or the knowledge if you like, that this was not the case, took us by surprise.

You work with the Filmverlag der Autoren, which is certainly a collective. How long have you had your films with them?

Since they started.

Do you give all your films to them?

Yes, even the ones I originally gave to other distributors.

Other directors don't do that.

I think it's sad that all German directors don't do it, that when a film of theirs turns out to be a success, they give it to another distributor...

...and only give the garbage to the Filmverlag...

Yes, the garbage that nobody else wants.

You don't do that as a matter of principle?

Right. As far as I'm concerned, the only realistic hope, even with filmmakers, is solidarity.

The actors in your films often use their real names.

The attitude I might have about my characters is related to the way I feel about the actors. I felt a certain way about Hanna Schygulla, so she is actually almost always the heroine, but also the traitor and who knows what else. I might have such an attitude about Irm Hermann, or Harry Baer, and for this reason, I usually give these people their own names. In spite of this I've tried to create stories in which these actors couldn't play themselves. It isn't true that I tell stories that might have been possible in the real lives of the actors.

They're fictional stories.

Fictional stories, in which, certainly, the yearnings of these people, their desires, their visions of utopia, exist as something real in the characters, but not in the story itself. I also have an attitude about these people as actors. From the beginning I've directed and filmed the actors as if they were stars.

Warhol has said that everyone is a star.

Yes, I agree, but I don't think someone is automatically a star just because of being placed in front of a camera, but only in a specific role, in a specific shot, in a specific camera movement. If the camera isn't Hollywood, then the actor being photographed isn't Hollywood. We've always attempted to be professional in our approach, even when we didn't have the means to do so; we've always tried to work as if we already had all the necessary technical and financial means at our disposal.

Why do you use so many actors who are familiar from the German films of the 50s and 60s: Karlheinz Bohm, Joachim Hansen...

That's a very logical development, of course. If I turn Hanna Schygulla into Marlene Dietrich, it follows that one day I'll want to hire Dietrich herself. And if I can't get her, I'd take, perhaps, Barbara Valentin, because in my opinion these actors have glamour. What it comes down to is that I believe I can work substantially better with them.

Why?

Because they're not so green...

You mean that older actors are more professional?

More professional and have a certain glamour, which I respect. They were always good; they only acted in bad films.

Have you ever tried to get a famous Hollywood star for one of your films?

Yes, Lana Turner.

Why couldn't you get her?

She wanted too much money.

For which film did you want her? Have you made the film?

No. I wanted to tell the same story that Sirk told in *All that Heaven Allows,* the story about the gardener.

But your film would have taken place in Germany?

Yes.

Your work methods are considered a great mystery. You've made about twenty features in five years, and in one year, 1970, six. How would you characterize this ability to produce so much more than other directors?

I can only say once again that I work my eight to twelve hours a day without pause, as others also have done. This naturally has psychological roots, which lie somewhere in my background, why, I don't know. But it is true, for instance, that I have to deal with everything that I experience in one way or another, in order to have the feeling that I've really experienced it.

It's natural, then, that you get a great deal done, the plays and radio shows, and of course, the films. It reminds me of someone like John Ford, who directed about 120 films, out of which perhaps twenty still have something to offer us. He certainly produced an immense body of work, but those twenty have survived. Would you say that this is the way you operate?

Yes, for the most part, up until now, I've preferred to make more, rather than bigger, things.

But still, they are very personal films, "auteur" films. In spite of that, they have a utilitarian character, a momentary quality.

Yes, because they are for the most part films to be thrown away—films that were made in a specific situation for a specific reason, and which therefore, as far as I'm concerned, can subsequently be forgotten. Up to now, I really haven't felt that "longing for immortality." Certainly, *Gods of the Plague* is a fairly accurate film about the feelings that actually existed during that strange postrevolutionary period around 1970. And *Beware of a Holy Whore* is also a fairly accurate film about groups, and has something timeless about it.

This quality of usefulness can also be formulated somewhat theoretically. Most of the directors in the New German Cinema see themselves as "authors" in the sense of being like poets, or maybe painters, while people like Ford or Hitchcock or Hawks or even yourself seem to have a concept of film which has more to do with architecture, in that an architect is not a "free" artist, but someone who works on commission. He gets a hundred orders, and perhaps ten or twenty of them allow him to express himself.

I think that's quite good.

A kind of handicrafts concept?

What do you mean by handicrafts? Architects make something very habitable.

Right. They produce for existing needs. An architect works on the principle that not all needs, even when they are distorted by manipulation, are totally false needs, but that a kernel of genuine need remains, which must be met at all costs. Then, something has been accomplished that is really useful to people.

I'd look at it that way, too.

Even in your films?

Yes.

If you are revealing your entire biography in your films, that means, naturally, that you will be making many more films in your life.

That I don't know.

Do you see it more as a problem in your personal life or in your film career?

It has something to do with my life, certainly, but it's clear that though filmmaking isn't everything to me, it's very important... I'm always having the feeling that I don't want to do it any more at all, that I'd like to take a break for a year or so, and then, when the first week of that year is up, I can't endure it any more after all; then I read something or other in the news, or someone tells me a story, and I know the second I hear it what must happen now. For me, it has always been very important to do a thing right away, without thinking about possible losses , and without making this "claim to eternity." It's just this story that I have to make now. For the most part, I guess we've taken unbelievable risks financially, so that after the first three films we made—*Love Is Colder than Death, Katzelmacher* and *Gods of the Plague*—which were all made totally without money, only with loans, we were 500,000 DM in debt, which we had to pay back, and to continue to make films, we always had to risk going under. Even now with *Effi Briest,* I've simply put everything I earned in the last three or four years into it, but I don't have to get it back with *Effi*—what I have to do, again with *Effi,* is find opportunities to earn money again somewhere else. And then, I simply have to trust even more that I can continue somehow or other.

Is Effi Briest your first film with a "claim to eternity"?

Yes, it certainly has more of a "claim to eternity" than any of the other films.

When did you become acquainted with Sirk's films?

In the Winter of 1970-71 in Munich, and then I went to see him in Ascona because I was absolutely gone on his films.

Were his films a further confirmation of things that you already believed?

They are all films which I would like to have made, but at the same time I think that mine are not like his.

Effi Briest ➤

You sought him out?

Yes, I visited him, to see how anyone is, who makes such films.

And how is he?

Someone completely refined, very clever, tough, well-informed... intellectual.

You have written that Sirk's films are "films by someone who loves people and doesn't despise them like we do." What did you mean by "like we do"?

"Like we do" means anyone who makes films in this part of the world.

In this part of the world. Would you include late Chabrol?

Not unconditionally for late Chabrol, no, but now that I've seen *Docteur Popaul* and *Nada,* I have my doubts about him.

La Decade Prodigeuse by Chabrol is so full of caricatures, and that's something you don't accept...

...which I don't accept. I'm against caricatures, and I'm against parody, but Chabrol before that, from *Les Biches* on...

In other words, La Femme Infidele, Que La Bete Meure, Le Boucher, La Rupture, Juste Avant la Nuit and Les Noces Rouges...

In exactly these films, though I think Sirk loves people more than Chabrol does, I'll admit Chabrol loves them enough in these films.

He loves them, but he criticizes them too, naturally.

Sirk does, too. I wouldn't say that in *Imitation of Life,* Sirk treats Lana Turner, or anyone else, uncritically, even the black mammy. When they call this film kitsch, that really infuriates me, because it's so stupid.

Maybe it is kitsch, but only to the extent that kitsch is in a certain sense precisely more real than official art.

That's probably true.

The fact that you make such simple films and concern yourself with trivial plots, however, is undoubtedly related to your attitude toward official art, which is that the official, acknowledged methods through which it expresses reality is untruthful.

I believe that official art is only qualified to suppress people.

Aren't there some caricaturish scenes in your own films, for example, in American Soldier, *when the maid commits suicide and the others pass by her as if it were nothing. Isn't that caricature?*

For me that wasn't a caricature. The point of that scene was to show how coldly people react when someone does something totally desperate. If this turns into parody, however, then I acknowledge it, and then I'm ashamed and excuse myself.

And Eight Hours Are Not a Day *isn't at least partly a parody of television series?*

No. What might be seen as parody is actually where my taste coincides with that of other TV series writers. I'm not doing parody—we actually have very similar attitudes.

But don't your early films contain a kind of parody that makes everything look like role-playing?

Parody, no. It is true that all the gangsters in the film are playing roles, because there are no gangsters in Germany.

No doubt there are some, but they don't run around that way.

Yes. I mean roles from Hollywood films.

Were there actually people who ran around like that in Germany at that time?

Yes, precisely, among people who saw themselves as gangsters. These people get their ideas about gangsters from these (Hollywood) films—the way they dress, their style, and then, as far as possible, they parody it in their lives, if you want to put it that way, but I don't find it a parody, I find it much sadder than that. These are people who take on roles that aren't really their own in order to participate in a life that seems worth living to them, and that is naturally very sad, or even very beautiful, if you like.

You are occasionally criticized for denigrating humanity in your films.

I would have to defend myself against charges of denigrating people in any of my films. On the contrary, I think I actually criticize humanity less than most other people do, and accept certain things much too readily, when it is really no longer feasible. For instance, when the father in *Jail Bait* talks about his wartime experiences, when his opinions become particularly obnoxious, I deal with him in an especially sensitive way, in order to make it clear that while his ideas may be loathsome, the man himself can be someone vulnerable and even loving. It's what he thinks and says that's terrible, not what he is.

When you say that you are less critical than other people, do you mean less than other German directors?

Less than most people who work in this country, yes.

But aren't there others, besides Sirk?

Of course, I know of many directors in the world who have a relationship with their characters that I find very beautiful.

Would you characterize this relationship as one in which the director doesn't place himself on a higher plane than his characters? In which he doesn't comment on them but understands and accepts them, so to speak, on his own level?

Right. Ultimately, he should be like them. He should admit to himself that at the very least, he is very like his characters.

But it is still possible to criticize the characters in such a way that it might be tantamount to self-criticism?

Right, yes.

Then the film would not, as is the case with most German directors, be made from an outside perspective...

...but from the inside...

By explaining the contradictions within the characters themselves?

Yes, a dialectical process, if you like.

The characters are not illustrations of contradictions, but are themselves subject to contradictions.

They suffer from contradictions that come instead from within. I've always said that I have no desire to make films about prototypes or ideologies, because I only know people—I have no idea about anything but human beings, if I know anything at all. I personally can't deal with models and the like in my work, any more than I can in real life.

Your older films contain many self-references, while your recent ones seem to be more objective. Is Beware of a Holy Whore *a turning point? Could it be said by any chance about this film that here you've dispersed yourself into a number of characters, in the same way that Don Quixote and Sancho Panza are two sides of the same person?*

I can't deny that, though I think some of the earlier films were more precise self-references. I think *Holy Whore* is above all the representation of a group, almost like an analysis of group behavior, while I'd consider *Love Is Colder than Death, Gods of the Plague, Rio das Mortes,* and also parts of *Whity* and *American Soldier,* more accurate self-portrayals. I would say that actually, each character is a part of me, even though they contradict one another to some extent. In *Holy Whore,* I began something really new, whereas I still find in *Pioneers in Ingolstadt* a bit of the old stuff, and though *Holy Whore* was really the last anti-teater film, *Pioneers* was made later. The films I've done since are actually just as autobiographical, if you want. Between *Pioneers* and *Merchant of the Four Seasons,* there was a period of almost a year when I didn't make any films, during which time I discovered a way to approach autobiography less onanistically, less as an end in itself, and possibly to find out what I could say about myself that would be more universally valid. Thus I began to see myself in relation to the outside world, and not just in relation to myself and my friends, and that, as far as I'm concerned, is the crucial distinction between the anti-teater films and the later films, which will certainly be a new phase, if I'm lucky enough to be able to work and I live long enough.

If Beware of a Holy Whore *signifies a change, doesn't* Merchant of the Four Seasons *indicate still another change?*

In *Holy Whore* something old comes to an end and something new begins, and in *Merchant,* that new thing is there.

...that one could call realism?

I still would never say "realism." I would say that the films have become more universal, that they are no longer just films for myself and my friends, but have become films for humanity, and so, they don't have the arrogance that the earlier films had. I think the films we made earlier, even though they were simpler than the recent ones, were more arrogant and cold. On the other hand, the later films are much more human, even if they are colder in terms of technical perfection. The most technically perfect films, in my opinion, are Sirk's, and in spite of that, they are the most human I know of.

Your newer films are not, naturally, realistic in the sense of being exact representations of exterior reality.

The realism which I care about and want is what happens in the head of the spectator and not what is on the screen. On the whole, that doesn't interest me; people get that every day. What I want is a more open realism, which allows and doesn't challenge the reality that people make for themselves. When you show people the same old experiences they're used to, they get bored, I think. Possibilities must be offered for people to open themselves up to beautiful things.

In Chabrol's La Rupture, *the main character is a woman, which is good. I believe that Chabrol could only express this beauty and the power of kindness through mad exaggeration, through which he produced a perfect world. He had to transform reality into a fable in order to express the simple fact that goodness is something beautiful, and a strength. If he had tried to make this statement "realistically," the audience would only have laughed and called it kitsch, and therefore, unbelievable.*

That's right. The more real things get, the more like myths they become. There have always been myths, but the myths of earlier times were, I'm convinced, bad ones, because they made people sick. So certainly, if we can tell evil stories to make people sick, we can also tell good myths that will make them well.

In a way, your films Merchant of the Four Seasons, Eight Hours Are Not a Day *and* Fear Eats the Soul *are like fables.*

I can say that the "unrealistic" in these films can bring people closer to their own reality, and beyond that, to a utopia, because they offer the possibility of recognition and because they don't hit people over the head with the same old thing. People don't want to see the same things; they want to experience their reality in a way that offers opportunities and doesn't obstruct them from having fun with their own reality. These didactic, mostly socialist, films take away people's pleasure in their own reality.

In your films you emphasize the essential to the detriment of the trivial. In reality, it would take a maid half an hour to bringing a steak to a hotel room, but in American Soldier, *it is brought almost immediately—that's unimportant, but if a worker in* Eight Hours Are Not a Day *takes a position of individualism or solidarity, that is important.*

Yes. I emphasize what I consider important for people and their potential.

What you consider important, however, seems often thoroughly identical with the objective tendencies of historical development, and is to that extent quite realistic.

Generally speaking, history doesn't interest me. What interests me is what I can understand about my possibilities and impossibilities, my hopes and utopian dreams, and how these things relate to my surroundings, that interests me. I'm interested in solidarity, and the potential I might have to overcome the things that bother me, fear and all that, much more than theory. I don't think theory is important to me as a TV watcher, but only as a reader of books. As a television or film spectator, what's important to me is what can activate my dreams in one way or another.

Since Merchant of the Four Seasons, *even the language in your films has changed. It's no longer the typical "Fassbinder-talk" we've been accustomed to since* Katzelmacher.

I've discovered for myself over the years that this language

Eight Hours are Not a Day

from the early films stands between the spectator and the film, and that the audience found the films inaccessible precisely because of the language; that Fassbinder-talk actually obstructed their access to the films. What I used to do with language I'm now trying to inject into the structure of the camera movements and the images, because I also believe that it is more successful in working upon the feelings of the audience as a beautiful and precise, but still very alien language.

But even now, the language is not totally equalized; it isn't identical with ordinary language.

It's always a very foreshortened, and also very stylized, language, but it is shortened and stylized in a different way than before.

In what way?

Earlier, the language I used appeared as something artificial,

whereas now that's not so obvious. I think this obvious artificiality in the language denies the audience access to the
narrative and I'm trying now to find ways to still allow for
definite peculiarities in the language for the characters, so as
not to block access to the film, but to expand the imagination
of the audience to what they receive from images and
dreams.

*You once said, "I want to create a distancing from things
that will give the possibility of becoming concerned with
those things." Is that generally true of your work?*

Generally, I would say yes. I would hope that the spectators
of film or television could have the chance to activate their
own feelings about the characters, but nevertheless, that the
possibility for reflection might be given in the structure of the
text itself, so that there is a distancing that might lend itself to
reflection.

In Martha *you followed the model of the Hollywood
psychological-horror film very closely. Still, the film is, you
might say, staged against the genre.*

It really couldn't be done otherwise. I just couldn't make a
film like Hitchcock's *Marnie* as *Marnie* is told, because I
don't have the courage for such naivete, simply to make such
a film and then at the end to give such an explanation. I don't
have that something which is a natural part of courage, but
maybe some day I will have it, and then I'll be just like Hollywood.

*The question is, really, whether that's what you want. Do
you want a German Hollywood?*

Yes.

Really?

Yes, I'm all for it. I want that absolutely.

For the most part, though, Hollywood films don't have a critical, but an affirmative function. Shouldn't films be made, as most media theory today suggests, against those cliches? You did, in the beginning, especially in your theatre.

Yes. I've changed, I guess. The best thing I can think of would be to create a union between something as beautiful and powerful and wonderful as Hollywood films and a criticism of the status quo. That's my dream, to make such a German film—beautiful and extravagant and fantastic, and nevertheless able to go against the existing order, like some Hollywood mass-films which are in no way apologies for the establishment, as is always superficially maintained. An example would be *Suspicion,* by Hitchcock, the most drastic film against the bourgeois institution of marriage I know.

But in any event, you don't want to make "art films" in the traditional sense, but rather, a kind of people's art?

Yes.

In the past few days, you've seen almost all your films. Looking back over your development, would you say that you've surmounted certain things and conquered others?

Yes, but that's an open question for me, because it's something that I'll have to think about just now. I've seen twenty-two films in four days. These are things I have to take into account for myself now.

The above text is taken from a five-hour taped interview conducted in Berlin on February 20, 1974. Supplementary questions were asked during another interview on March 10, 1974. Wilhelm Roth participated in the Berlin discussion.

Fassbinder's Reality: an Imitation of Life

By Ruth McCormick

In psychoanalysis, only the exaggerations are true.

Theodor W. Adorno

Fassbinder's 1979 film *The Third Generation* is "Dedicated to a true lover, and therefore, probably, to nobody." His first full-length film is called *Love Is Colder than Death;* Marie, the heroine of his second, *Katzelmacher,* tells her Greek lover, "I know I love you, because it hurts so much"; Jeff, the director in *Beware of a Holy Whore,* is accused by more than one other character of being "incapable of love"; Hans' sister in *Merchant of the Four Seasons* tells his small daughter that he is unhappy because "no one has loved him enough"; Hanni, the rebellious teenager who urges her boyfriend to kill her father in *Jail Bait* declares after his trial, "It wasn't real love with us, it was just physical"; Petra von Kant, when Karin deserts her, screams, "I loved her!"; Effi Briest confesses on her deathbed that the harsh, unforgiving husband who ruined her life was "right all along"—that he was "as good as a man could be, who is without love"; a 1976 television drama about a repressed young man who cracks up and kills a man he thinks is his father is entitled *I Only Want You to Love Me.* In Fassbinder's films, the characters talk about love continually, but even where love may have a chance for survival *(Eight Hours Are Not a Day, Fear Eats the Soul),* it faces tremendous odds. Che Guevara once said that the revolutionary must be motivated by feelings of great love. Love is, for Fassbinder, the utopian moment in the process of change, both political and personal, the impossible which must be made possible by a radical upheaval in human attitudes. How this upheaval is to come about is never mentioned: rather, Fassbinder's films are like a litany of the the failures of love in the world.

Most love scenes in Fassbinder's films are cold, even repugnant. In the early films, only in *Katzelmacher*, do we see any genuine affection, and this is between Marie and Jorgos (the other sexual relationships in the film are absolutely dismal). Only when we get to *Beware of a Holy Whore* do we find another love scene which could in any way be described as sensual, let alone tender, and this one also features Hanna Schygulla (with Eddie Constantine). In *Pioneers in Ingolstadt*, there are also moments of real warmth between Hanna Schygulla and Harry Baer, which make her eventual desertion all the more moving. In fact, with the exception of those depicting the Emmi-Ali relationship in *Fear Eats the Soul*, every scene that could be properly called a "love scene" in Fassbinder's films involves Hanna Schygulla (others being those between Maria Braun and the black soldier Bill, and Willie and Robert in the first part of *Lili Marleen.*) There are flickers of love between Hanni and Franz in *Jail Bait*, Petra von Kant and Karin, and Franz and Eugen in *Fox and His Friends,* but these all occur at the beginning of their relationships, and are quickly extinguished. Bolwieser and Hermann in *Despair* lust after their wives, but because of their obsessions, what might have been sensual becomes merely ridiculous. Some of the most chilling scenes in Fassbinder's films take place when two people go to bed together—Ricky and the prostitute Rosa in *American Soldier,* Hans and Irmgard (and Irmgard and Anzell) in *Merchant of the Four Seasons,* Margot and the pharmacist in *Fear of Fear,* Walter and Andree in *Satan's Brew,* Ariane and her lover in *Chinese Roulette,* and Paul and Hilde in *The Third Generation.* If love is well-nigh impossible for Fassbinder's characters, sex is usually a drag.

Is Fassbinder trying to say that modern life is absolute hell? That there are no happy marriages, families, friendships? Is it only Germany that has come to this sad state? As has been noted many times, Fassbinder's "world" is not a carbon-copy of the real one. If Ozu, for example, gives us a recognizable world, in which, although his Japanese subjects have different customs from ours, we can identify the things that happen and the conversations of the characters as close to our own daily lives, Fassbinder gives us a world that is always at least a bit exaggerated, always strange. Through the camera, we become invisible witnesses to events that could take place, but never "really" do in the way they do in a Fassbinder film. Situations are extreme, as are emotions, although they are not incredible. They are within the realm of possibility, but usually confirm our worst suspicions. Nobody behaves quite as outrageously as Walter Kranz in *Satan's Brew,* even avant-garde poets—or do they? After all, we all know that poets can be egomaniacs, and Kranz is from the land of mad artists and crazy political movements. The Christ(!) family in *Chinese Roulette* are rich and elegant, but the crippled daughter can't stand her parents, who seem to regard her as an intruder who has destroyed their love life. Their housekeeper's son plagiarizes philosophical texts, but only the daughter is well-educated enough to realize that his "writings" are not original. The mute governess bears the same name as their Franconian castle. A blind beggar comes to the door, and then drives away in a Mercedes, which both the lady of the house and her servant find amusing. Crazy? Isn't it true that many parents regard their children as inconveniences, that many children have contempt for their parents, that a good deal of "serious" writing today only rehashes work that has been done before, that the *nouveau riche* are buying up the castles of impoverished aristocrats, that just about everything is a ripoff of one kind or another? And there may be more love in *our* world than in Fassbinder's, but surely not enough, or the world wouldn't be in the terrible mess it's in.

Fassbinder does not pretend to be original, although he combines elements of his cinematic models, from Hollywood gangster films and melodramas, from favorite directors (Sirk, Walsh, Sternberg, Hawks, Bunuel, Visconti, Rohmer, Godard, Chabrol, et. al.) with Freudian-Marxist-Frankfurt School social theories in a way that makes him unique among contemporary filmmakers. His films bear the mark of an *auteur,* and, despite the many developments and refinements of his style, his concerns have remained consistent from the early "gangster" films through *Berlin Alexanderplatz* and *Lili Marleen.* In fact, *Berlin Alexanderplatz,* Alfred Doblin's monumental novel of a *lumpen* hero who dreams of love and respectability, which he was finally able to make as a 15 1/2-hour, 14-part television series in 1980, had fascinated him since he first read it when he was sixteen. This story of one man's failure to find his utopia, written and situated in the years before the rise of Hitler, appealed to him personally and in the long run, politically. Franz Biberkopf's obsessive attraction to the psychopathic Reinhold appeared to the young man, who was trying to deal with his own emerging homosexuality, as a revelation. Biberkopf's loss of his beloved Mieze and of his optimistic ideals, which were the product of a false consciousness, seem to foreshadow Fassbinder's own belief that happiness and fulfillment are impossible in a society which propagates false notions of love and success. The failure of Franz Biberkopf could, in fact, be read as the failure of Germany itself. In any case, its basic themes and characters are repeated time and again in Fassbinder's films: personal and political failure are seen as one and the same. The pessimism of these films echoes that of Marcuse's *One-Dimensional Man* and Horkeimer and Adorno's *Dialectic of the Enlightenment*. Like these thinkers, Fassbinder cannot name the unnameable, the better society, but insists upon the importance of the utopian imagination in its realization. If Mao Zedong cautions against "incorrect thinking," Fassbinder warns against "incorrect feeling."

If one theme is consistent in all Fassbinder's films, from the early, rather misogynist "gangster" films on, it is that victims internalize their own oppression, either by clinging to false, socially-determined ideas of what they should want, or by yearning for a leader, a lover, a master—someone who will make things right for them. Fassbinder's characters, like a depressing number of us, want to be led whether we realize it or not, want to be told what to think and how to feel, want to feel "loved." The first form of internalized oppression, the yearning for the "good life" we see in films and on television, hear about from our parents and friends, and read about in books and magazines, is blatantly obvious in almost all Fassbinder's films; the second, the desire for domination, is more subtle, but stands in direct relation to the first. The young gangsters in *Love Is Colder than Death*, *Gods of the Plague* and *American Soldier* are right out of *Berlin Alex-*

Martha

anderplatz, though their outward mannerisms are out of American gangster films. The "hero" of the first two films mentioned is named Franz Walsch (a bow to Raoul), and, like Biberkopf, he only wants to get together enough money to go straight and marry his girlfriend Joanna, a prostitute with bourgeois dreams. However, he allows his more streetwise friend Bruno to lure him back into working for the syndicate. Joanna/Mieze is no longer seen as an "angel," but as a possessive woman who wants to trap Franz into a dull middle-class existence, while Bruno/Reinhold, who models himself on Humphrey Bogart (or Alain Delon as Humphrey Bogart), represents a kind of freedom, however warped. The end is the same; there is no escape for Franz, no real happiness with either the man or the woman he loves. Although the film is crude, displaying political naivete in its implication that a life outside "the system" side-by-side with Bruno is preferable to a "conventional" life with Joanna, there is really no alternative to be seen; each choice only offers its own kind of prison. The hoods who ape the gangsters in American films are as incapable of real life as the women who dream of the joys of married life. Fassbinder has laid out his word-view right here, and it has yet to be changed.

"Franz Biberkopf," the seeker of love and freedom, appears many times and in many guises in Fassbinder's films, and continually meets with the same failure. Jorgos, the Greek worker in *Katzelmacher*, hopes to make a better life for himself in Germany, and even though he left a wife and two kids in Greece, wants to include the romantic Marie in his plans. Simple common sense tells us he will fail, just as his German counterparts have already failed. Kurt R in *Why Does Herr R Run Amok?* has a life Franz and Jorgos might envy—a professional job, a home, a pretty wife, a young son, respectability. It is the prison that drives him insane. All Hans in *Merchant of the Four Seasons* wanted out of life was some love and some freedom; he might as well have asked for the stars. Franz, the unemployed carnie of *Fox and His Friends*, suddenly wins a huge lottery and meets the man of his dreams, but because he's completely unaware of what makes the world go 'round (and it's not love), he ends up far worse off than when he started; along with his "love" and his money, he finally loses his illusions. Erwin Weishaupt, an orphan, becomes a woman, Elvira, for the sake of the man he loves. The sacrifice is totally ignored. He tries to return to his wife and daughter, but it is too late. No one understands a word he says, and there is no longer any place for him in the world.

In these films, form serves content in an amazingly effective way. So much has been written about Fassbinder's stylistic devices, his mirror shots in which the characters experience themselves as the "other," his framing devices, which seem to isolate and/or imprison the dramatis personae in their constricted worlds, the jarring closeups and clinical overhead shots, that to write more at this point seems superfluous. What the stories and dialogue have already made evident is "brought home" even more forcefully by the actual look of the films. In *In a Year of 13 Moons*, Elvira Weishaupt lives in such a dark world that when she ventures into the sunlight, we are almost blinded. This is, indeed, a world where nuns and suicides would be reading Schopenhauer, where the intrusion of the culture industry into a depressing apartment via television seems even more deadening than it otherwise would. On the other hand, Willie in *Lili Marleen* is almost always bathed in light. As a performer, this is her element, but the light gets stronger the closer she gets to the Nazi hierarchy, and becomes an ironic epiphany when she is ushered into Der Fuhrer's office. In the end, when she is deserted by her love, she walks off into the darkness. The terrorists in *The Third Generation* operate in darkness, surrounded by sounds they never seem to notice from a variety of electronic devices; this would seem to reflect the darkness and chaos in their own heads.

Only Fassbinder tells stories like this, and does it with dazzling proficiency. He has gathered around him a number of the most gifted people working in cinema today. As a result, he is probably the most successful of the directors in "new German cinema." He is certainly the most controversial; his films have been called "provocations," and he is probably delighted about that. He has said that he would like to make psychoanalysis available to those who can't afford it, and, like a good analyst, he uses a sometimes-painful Socratic method. It is as if he were trying to blast away the preconditioning of his audience by showing them themselves (and himself in the bargain) through the mirror of cinema. He is "provoking" everyone who has bought time-honored promises of happiness, whether they be fellow leftists who thought that demonstrating, organizing, making "revolutionary" art, and "educating" the oppressed through pamphlets and documentaries, would somehow bring about instant utopia, as well as conservative and apolitical men and women who still believe the advertisements, who expect "love" as part of their birthright, along with a good job, plenty of money, security, freedom and fun. Fassbinder's characters are paradigms for us all. They have all bought the promises of the consumer society, and when their dreams don't come true, they see themselves as cheated, betrayed. For some of these "Biberkopfs"—Hans, Fox, Elvira, Herr R and possibly, Maria Braun, it is more than they can bear, and they kill themselves. Effi Briest, whose possibilities are more limited by the time in which she lives, simply fades away, while Martha, who has totally internalized her masochism, seems even happy when she she must ultimately face a life of complete dependency.

While psychological oppression is constantly evident in these films, the social oppression of his characters is seldom shown as clearly. True, the surroundings of the characters in *Katzelmacher* and the early gangster films are tacky and depressing; Jorgos and Ali are obvious victims of racist prejudice, as is Elvira of the kind of "macho" prejudice sometimes suffered by transsexuals and "queens" in the gay community; the shocking conditions under which the young Franz must work are shown in *Jail Bait*. But it is often seen as a weakness in Fassbinder's films that more concrete forms of oppression are not seen, but take a back seat to more psychological forms of repression. Oppressed people are often depicted as victims of their own peers (immigrant workers by German workers in *Katzelmacher* and *Fear Eats the Soul;* homosexuals by other homosexuals in *Fox and His Friends* and *In a Year of 13 Moons,* and women by other women in *The Bitter Tears of Petra von Kant, Fear of Fear,* and *Women in New York).* Even a child becomes an oppressor (though, we suspect, with good reason) in *Chinese Roulette.* Mother Kusters is treated with almost as little sensitivity by her children and the "well-meaning" radicals as she is by the yellow press, and we are hard put to know who is oppressing the terrorists in *The Third Generation.* Even their "alienation" and political ideas are never articulated. We do know, however, that their personal lives, for the most part, are not very happy. They seem to have lost the utopian vision which had inspired earlier generations of revolutionaries, who were at least capable of ideas, and who asked questions that have yet to be answered.

At one point in *The Third Generation,* someone remarks, "The masses create their exploiters," not realizing that the group is itself being exploited for the benefit of U. S. business interests. These "rebels without a cause," isolated from the "masses" for whom they say they are fighting, are as much sitting ducks for the establishment as any of Fassbinder's deluded petty-bourgeois conformists. If Fassbinder has been criticized for anything, it has been for his lack of "sympathy" for the oppressed—for women, workers, gays, and in a *cause celebre* (*Garbage, the City and Death/Shadows of Angels*), Jews—even more than for his criticisms of the "left" in Germany. The implications that are drawn by Fassbinder's critics, and that they, in turn, believe will be drawn by bigots, sexists, and conservatives of various stripes, are that women, workers, gays, Jews, etc., are not only responsible for their plight, but are, in the long run, no better than their oppressors. It is gay immigrant workers, people doubly oppressed, who beat Elvira in *In a Year of 13 Moons* when they find she is not just a transvestite, but a transsexual. Then, her male lover leaves her because she has gotten "fat and stupid." Elvira's own seeming masochism can lead to the conclusion that she deserves what she gets. Seitz, the heterosexual for whom Elvira had his operation, spent time in a concentration camp and subsequently made a fortune exploiting others. Is he a Jew? That is not as important as the fact that, as Elvira explains to a friendly prostitute, he was so warped by his experiences that a brothel he owned was called Bergen-Belsen. The prostitute later meets Seitz, and is totally charmed by him. We can't help suspecting that Robert Mendelsson's rich, aristocratic father in *Lili Marleen* disapproves of his son's engagement to a cabaret singer as much for the reason that she's "not the right sort" (not rich, not Jewish) as because she is German. Petra von Kant assumes a "male" role in her attempted domination of Karin, who in turn adopts a "conniving female" role. Eugen, true to his class, exploits poor Franz and then throws him out, but it cannot be said that Franz is not at least partially to blame for his own downfall. He has been inordinately stupid about his money, and has made very little effort to make any changes in his lumpen lifestyle to please the man he says he loves. It cannot, however, be said, that Fassbinder does not consider himself as much at fault as other people in the perpetuation of domination. Implicitly in *Beware of a Holy Whore* and *Satan's Brew* and explicitly in *Germany in Autumn,* he has shown himself as a quasi-oppressor. It is very disturbing to see the latter film now, in view of the subsequent suicide of Armin Meier, the recipient of Fassbinder's tirades, but it adds to our feeling that he is trying very hard to be honest about himself, as well as about the human condition. It is

In a Year of 13 Moons

possible that his insistence upon showing the all-pervasive
master-slave syndrome in modern society leads to his being
misunderstood, but even the anger and controversy that are
raised by his treatment of social problems perhaps bring
more attention to them than a good-guys-bad-guys approach, as common in most leftist films as in Hollywood,
ever could. If the oppressed become oppressors, or if they
passively accept their oppression, Fassbinder seems to be saying, they are suffering from a failure of imagination.

In an article on German cinema in *Vogue* (Oct., 1980),
critic Andrew Sarris reports that he was taken to task by a
disgruntled journalist from *Der Spiegel* for admiring any of
Fassbinder's films after *Merchant of the Four Seasons,*
because "people like Fassbinder are responsible for the
Baader-Meinhof gang." It seems to me that this unhappy
(and probably conservative) journalist is putting the cart
before the horse. Like the young extremists in *The Third
Generation*, Fassbinder is a child of the 'sixties. His contemporaries in Germany—and the rest of the world—who are
making art in the 'seventies and 'eighties are seldom much

more thrilled with the status quo than he is. The old, optimistic "social realism" of earlier leftist artists has virtually disappeared, except in a few documentaries and in what we've been able to see coming out of the People's Republic of China, and in the other aesthetic camp, even Godard is edging away from the neo-formalism of his 'seventies work, and Straub/Huillet are rediscovering their sense of humor. Fassbinder's "exaggerated" stories, his increasing irony, his fluctuating between the things he likes best about Hollywood films and ongoing stylistic investigations into new forms of cinematic language bespeak a need to communicate that is both personal and political. He is hardly promoting terrorism—only mirroring it. There is just as much alienation, and a good deal more violence, in the work of any number of American directors (Coppola, Scorsese, de Palma, Cimino, Peckinpagh, innumerable "gore 'n' horror" directors) than in Fassbinder's films, and much less social analysis or insight. Can an artist pretend to see happiness and promise where they don't exist? Fassbinder, like other German directors of his generation, sees a damaged society, totally dominated by technology and utilitarian rationality, obsessed with quantity to the detriment of quality, in which the corporately-controlled mass media try to sell us everything, even our dreams. Fassbinder's people are trapped and bombarded—perhaps more than we are—but that is what gives his films their cautionary power. These gangsters and terrorists, businessmen and housewives, Franz Biberkopfs and and Elvira Weishaupts, can't imagine things different from the way they are. The black man who hangs himself in *In a Year of 13 Moons* tells Elvira that he refuses to live a life that cannot be on his own terms; in a quote from Bresson's heartbreaking *Le Diable, Probablement*, the latest of Fassbinder's Franz Walsches deliberately walks into a police trap in a cemetery—there is nothing to live for now that his sweetheart and the revolution are both dead. However, there are moments of humor and tenderness in these films that say that all is not lost; their complexity and trickiness tell us to keep our eyes open; maybe things aren't as bad as they seem, if we employ all our faculties of thought, feeling, and especially, imagination. When the ruling class starts aping Jerry Lewis and getting itself kidnapped to increase sales, they're in trouble. The world changes.

Since Fassbinder is, by his own admission, both a highly subjective artist and an unrelenting critic of the status quo, can we separate the man—the product of progressive schooling and a broken home, the avowed homosexual and avid cinephile—from the artist—frenetically busy, innovative, disciplined—from the social critic who believes that we live in a totally dominated world, and that Western bourgeois art had already exhausted all its possibilites with Verdi's *La Traviata*? What Frederic Jameson says of Walter Benjamin in his book *Marxism and Form* holds equally true for Fassbinder: "How many modern philosophers have described the 'damaged existence' we lead in modern society, the psychological impairment caused by the division of labor and by specialization, the general alienation of modern life in all its aspects? Yet for the most part these analyses remain abstract; through them there speaks the resignation of the intellectual specialist to his own maimed present, the dream of wholeness, where it persists, attaching itself to someone else's future. Benjamin is unique among those thinkers in that he wants to save his own life as well..."

If Fassbinder's films are problematic, however, it is because of his dialectical imagination, which very often leads to ambiguity. As Richard Dyer points out in his article, "Reading Fassbinder's Sexual Politics" (*Fassbinder,* BFI, 1980, p. 54), the films "will be very differently understood by different members of the audience according to both their structural position in society (class, gender, race, sexual orientation, etc.) and their political orientation." They are, however, and I agree, "eminently suitable for further debate." The personal and the political are so intertwined, the relations between individuals are often so symbolic of larger social relations, that Fassbinder's films, more than those of most other directors, are important in dealing with the problem of communicating with a large mass audience without resorting to an unreal "social realism" or shifting over to the cliches of the culture industry, bombarding the spectator with images to the point where (s)he loses the capacity for critical thought. One should not have to read interviews with a director in order to understand her or his films. On the other hand, audiences do not want to be preached at; that is not good politics or good psychoanalysis.

If Fassbinder can be compared to Brecht, whom he considers too cerebral ("The rational doesn't interest me"), it is in his ability to force the viewer away from the subject-matter, to consider it, to feel emotions about it, and to have to take those feelings, as he says, back into the street. While he attracts an audience with the beauty of his films, with the skill of the actors, with the strangeness of the stories he tells, he challenges them to make up their own endings. Fassinder does not want to be co-opted into the system, as much as he wishes to make "Hollywood" films. So far, he seems to have avoided it, even in "popular" films like *Lili Marleen* and *The Marriage of Maria Braun*. At this point, he is the best known of the younger German directors, and has the easiest time raising money. He is considered "bankable." He is now considering projects like Freud's *The Man Moses* and Skinner's *Walden Two*. He is showing increasing comic gifts, and an ability to use them in a subversive way. Though it may be true that he offers no answers, he asks question after question. His life seems at much at stake as ours.

Franz, Mieze, Reinhold, Death and the Devil Rainer Werner Fassbinder's Berlin Alexanderplatz

by Wolfram Schutte

This Sunday (October 12, 1980) the first one-and-a-half-hour segment of *Berlin Alexanderplatz* will be shown on television at approximately 9:05 p.m., followed by one-hour segments every succeeding Monday evening at 9:30 p.m., culminating at 11:00 p.m. on December 29 with a dream sequence. With its 13 million DM production cost, its 100 leading and supporting actors, its 3,000 extras, its nine-month shooting schedule and almost 12-month production time, it is the most talked-about, most expensive and longest film project ever commissioned by German television. Even for its director-scriptwriter, who in the fourteen years of his artistic career (since 1965) has done over three dozen films, television series, theatrical presentations and radio plays—not exactly the laziest, most backward, least dedicated or least creative artist in Germany—even for such a dynamically productive author-director as Rainer Werner Fassbinder, this fifteen-and-a-half hour adaptation of Alfred Doblin's monumental novel of big-city life, *Berlin Alexanderplatz*, which was originally published in 1929 (when Doblin was 51 years old) is important as more than merely his longest piece of work. It is, for the present, the sum of his 33-year-long life: the great confession, the settlement of a debt, the fulfilment of a dream, and the summing up of all his previous artistic efforts.

Fassbinder first read the Doblin novel when he was 14 or 15 years old. He tells us this in an article he wrote when he was almost finished with the script. To begin with, he was not "turned on" by it. He knows why: "As a matter of fact, the author held himself back, perhaps out of cowardice, perhaps out of an unacknowledged nervousness about the traditional moral values of his class and times, perhaps out of an unconscious fear of some personal problem or other. Doblin avoids for many chapters, many many pages long, perhaps too many, his theme, or, better, the real theme of his novel, which is the meeting of the hero, Franz Biberkopf, with the other hero of the novel, Reinhold, a meeting which determines the later developments in the lives of both men." At this point, he became entangled with the book. "I wasn't reading any more, but rather, living, suffering, despairing, fearing." The book turned into a manual for living, a lifeline, for the "real dangers of puberty. It helped me to admit my tormenting fear, which almost crippled me, the fear of acknowledging my homosexual desires, of realizing my repressed needs; this book helped me to keep from becoming totally sick, mendacious, desperate. It helped me not to go to pieces."

Five years later, at twenty, he read the book again, and suddenly, in the middle, became aware "that an enormous part of myself, my attitudes, my reactions, so many things that I had considered all my own, were none other than those described by Doblin. I had...unconsciously made Doblin's fantasy my own life." A second-hand life, dictated by literature: an "I" invented by someone else. His terror is understandable.

"And yet," continues Fassbinder in the article, which appeared in the *Zeit* on March 14, 1980, "it was not in the long run...the novel which helped me to overcome subsequent crises of anxiety and to work on something which ultimately, as I hoped, relates very much to what is called an identity, insofar as is possible in all this messed-up garbage."

When he was asked later, after he had made his first films, why the hero was so often named Franz, he would mumble (in those days he was inhibited, not as eloquent as he is today), "It comes from Doblin's *Alexanderplatz*. I'd like to make a film of it some day." Then he himself played Franz Biberkopf, an unemployed carnival performer who wins a lottery and whose rich "boyfriend" spends all his money and then leaves him to die. Franz Biberkopf is the name of the hero of Fassbinder's first-comic, then tragic melodrama, *Fox and His Friends* (1975).

If *Berlin Alexanderplatz* was his compass during his adolescent years, Douglas Sirk's films have certainly become his

North Pole. Fassbinder's reading of the novel and his appropriation of the theme as the paradigm of his existential interpretation of life, tend toward melodrama.

Franz and Reinhold: "The story of two men whose little lives on this earth are destroyed because they never get the opportunity to muster up the courage even to recognize, much less to be able to admit to themselves, that they desire one another in an unusual way." (Fassbinder). Unclear, suppressed feelings, undeclared love, repression, aggression, violence, death. At the same time, Fassbinder's adolescent suspicion of latent homosexual tendencies in the curious relationship of Franz to Reinhold becomes—precisely because the two "are in no way homosexual"—transformed into the utopia of "pure love, not endangered by social convention." Accordingly, this love is not adulterated by financial transactions, sadistic dependency, marital battles; it is the "Absoluteness of Feeling" (Kleist); *Tristan and Isolde* is one of his favorite operas (he ought to direct it—where?). This yearning for love as a haven from social constraints and erotic determinism established more than his relationship to Sirk's highly-strung films; Fassbinder's own films are broken up by precisely this confusion, unfulfilment, defenselessness, in which this yearning for love sacrifices its heros and heroines. Indeed, the "Greek from Greece" in *Katzelmacher* (1969) is such a victim, *Fear Eats the Soul* (1973) is such a title, *I Only Want You to Love Me* (1976) is a cry for help, and *In a Year of 13 Moons* (1978) is an obituary.

Werner Schroeter has adapted this same passion for an exploding yearning for love through the use of everyday, artistic and cultural myths, ripping them out of everyday life through the power of music, so that this yearning for love is expressed in its purest form (wordlessly).

Fassbinder, on the other hand, looks for it among the "little people," and has found it in Doblin. Not only is his attitude the same (as Fassbinder's) when he strips the characters down to the barest details of their naked existence, enticing the reader through "the greatest tenderness", "ultimately to love" these mediocre people, but what is particularly important to the would-be idyll-maker Fassbinder in Doblin is "that precisely these apparently inconspicuous, unimportant, insignificant individuals, the so-called 'little people', are allowed the same 'greatness' that is customarily accorded only to the 'great'." Transportation workers, pimps, murderers, and the thief Franz Biberkopf are "granted the kind of differentiated subconscious, paired with an almost incredible fantasy life and capacity for suffering, as is not allowed so extensively to most characters in world literature."

This is a self-willed, subjective, even narcisstic, reading of a complex novel, an appropriation which projects into the work the desires, wishes, fears and utopian ideals of the reader, who discovers, emphasizes, accentuates, and coordinates trace elements of the author, incorporating them into his own vision. This is perfectly legitimate. Just as each spectator makes his or her own film from what is on the screen, so each reader writes his or her own book (mentally and emotionally).

In "the story of Franz Biberkopf," Doblin saw a morality tale about a "violent cure". Here is a good-natured but quick-tempered man, living in a time of unemployment, surrounded by pimps and criminals, whose ambition it is to be "respectable," to stand on his own two feet, and to rely on his own strength. "The wool must be pulled from his eyes," so that he is able to realize that his ideas about life were mistaken. He is "proud and unsuspecting, audacious, but at the same time timid and full of failings." Pride comes before the fall. Franz Biberkopf must be humiliated, that he may repent. Doblin, born a Jew, was at this time already well on the way to embracing Catholicism. This hustler-Quixote must empty his head of humbug, this lumpenproletarian hero must have his back broken. He must go through hell and rise again, cleansed, as Franz Karl Biberkopf. Reinhold the demon plays Mephistopheles in this scenario. Glorification of myth, parody of myth—at the point of intersection of these two concepts, Doblin locates the reason for the rise (and fall) of Biberkopf's "way of thinking."

Walter Benjamin saw in *Berlin Alexanderplatz* a "thieves' *Education Sentimentale,* the most extreme, most fraudulent, most advanced, final phase of the old bourgeois psychological novel."

Doblin's recently-deceased friend Robert Minder, who is one of the foremost experts on his work, considered the novel a "religious didactic poem," and Biberkopf, a German reincarnation of Michel whose "inner fears Doblin exposed" when he located the "erotic root" of Biberkopf's "decline of strength" in his relationship to Reinhold.

What did others say? Contemporary critics praised the novel as "the most advanced work of an epoch", which "allows the city of Berlin to speak in a thousand voices." The dogmatic Marxists of *Left Curve* considered Doblin's abstention from party politics a "shameless insult to German proletarian literature." Therefore, this "counterrevolutionary novel does not deserve to be read by the workers of the Soviet Union."

Today, the special position of the novel is uncontested. It is one of Doblin's masterpieces, the most important novel of big-city life in German literature—the most sweeping, richest summary of modern literary techniques, taking up and absorbing every imaginable modern, historical, mythical, religious testimony on writing and language, from popular texts on dialect and jargon to the Bible, from morality tales based on popular songs to technical scientific texts, and "lyrically, dramatically and reflectively" reviving the epics of Homer, Dante and Cervantes (Doblin). An ocean of a book, in which the little fish Biberkopf swims.

What will Fassbinder do with this "religious didactic poem", or with its fully orchestrated, Babylonian confusion of the many languages of a large modern city? With this *Song of Songs* of the Ego and this Requiem of its falling away to nothing? With this naturalistic reproduction of an era and its signs, rhythms, music, as well as the metaphysical ill-tidings of the human sacrifice of the man Biberkopf? With this fact-laden, topographically exact reproduction of Weimar Berlin with its inundated, atomized lives? What will Fassbinder do, not just with "the story of Franz Biberkopf" but with *Berlin Alexanderplatz?*

The "real" backdrop for the story was the region around the "Alex," the police station, the workers' neighborhood, the taverns and the back yards of Berlin as Doblin saw them when he practised there as a doctor (and which were familiar to Berliners who read the novel). This area is simply gone now; it has disappeared from the face of the earth, destroyed, annihilated. The novel is, therefore, something like a last extensive literary snapshot.

According to Fassbinder, a similar environment can be found in the Montparnasse section of Paris. At one time he had the idea of casting Gerard Depardieu as Biberkopf. Fassbinder wished to serve a double obsession, for television and film. He was, as always (unfortunately), disappointed.

The Bavaria Atelier Management Company, where Fassbinder's television sponsor Dieter Rohrbach and his scriptwriter Peter Martesheimer went for assistance, is very large and has an enormous capacity. Rohrbach, coiner of the slogan "amphibian film" (which can alternate from cinema to television, from television to cinema), had long dreamed of landing the biggest fish ever for television. Fassbinder took the bait: since he was twenty, he had been occupied with "plans to eventually dare to film this very special literature as an experiment with all the means at my disposal." Did the reality (the capacity of the Atelier) prompt the idea (of a big, long film), or did the idea (of many months of filming) prompt him to the reality (of a permanent workplace, where everything was set up)?

Fassbinder has consciously appropriated quotes from Doblin's novel many times (more often, he observes looking back on his work, than *unconsciously).* Many times, but Doblin, in his turn, used even more in his montage-novel—countless quotes, thousands of them. Why not then, since the real exteriors and original locales no longer exist, simply hint at them through "quotation"?

The first thirteen episodes (only the fourteenth, "My Dream of Franz Biberkopf's Dream''' shows definite signs of Fassbinder's interventions and additions) mix typical images of the times with the sound of the wheels of trains and the frenzied strains of Richard Tauber's rendition of the energetically stupefying popular-operetta song, "Oh Signora, Oh Signorina." These are invocations of the kind of colorful sound melanges characteristic of the era, thrown as it were upon an imaginary theatre curtain. In the background we see a studio-landscape, from which the film very seldom escapes, for example when Franz goes on an excursion to the country with his Mieze, or when she allows Reinhold to entice her to the same place, where he subsequently kills her.

Again, what has he done—with the big-city novel, I mean? He hasn't done anything with it. The few studio-made street scenes, filmed on the same set as Bergman's *The Serpent's Egg*, are properly shabby, but innocuous. But if he could, would Fassbinder have done something else? Didn't he want precisely this artificiality, at the risk of ending up with a theatrical decor? And has he given up the city as an iconographic backdrop in order to portray it so vigorously through sounds—language, dialect, music, radio?

And Doblin's montages-cum-collages? They are here, emphatically represented by inserts in the soundtrack. Doblin, the teller of moral tales and all-knowing author, is quoted by Fassbinder himself, sometimes over the images, sometimes by stopping the scene and interrupting the action. When we read Doblin, we have only the text, not his emphasis, his voice; we may assume irony, sarcasm, even (slightly) sadistic dominance when he siezes Biberkopf by the arm and upsets his plans, but here, Fassbinder speaks softly, sympathetically, lovingly, persuasively, tenderly. Only once, if I remember correctly, does he allow the two texts to speak simultaneously and become intertwined—when Biberkopf forces the sister of the woman he murdered (as a result of which he spent four years in prison) to sleep with him. Where Doblin inserted advertisements, newspaper announcements, *faits divers* which are, objectively speaking, part of the text, alongside the characters and the action, Fassbinder has Biberkopf find them and read them aloud, because in frequent moments of absentmindedness, moments of intense psychic pain, he has Franz deliver involuntarily-remembered words from airs and popular songs, which Doblin had interwoven as sneering dissonances, as scanning rhythms, into the texture of the book.

Fassbinder's grasp of the material is especially evident here. Though he doesn't gloss over the contradictions of the book in his film, he nevertheless cuts through the web of protests, digressions and commentaries, bringing them more closely in line with the story, weeding out for himself the primary narrative material from the original luxuriant, proliferating prose. He is the storyteller of people (among our directors, the greatest and most intensive).

This personal adaptation tends more than anything else toward a kind of re-psychologizing, however much he may restore a certain depth and breadth, a symphonic quality, to his condensation of the text by adopting Doblin's epic approach. Last but by no means least, there are the complex musical collages by Peer Raben. He has composed tiny symphonies and Masses, and developed continuing themes for Franz, Reinhold and Mieze. This is downright admirable (and also daring).

Not just the music, but also Fassbinder's interpretation, which maintains the undeclared, repressed love relationship between Franz and Reinhold as the central event of the novel, reinforces the transformation of the story into melodrama. What was for Doblin the "visible and invisible story" of the novel (his physics and metaphysics) is for Fassbinder the inner and outer aspects of his characters, a psycho-somatic dialectic.

The inner spaces of the characters predominate in Fassbinder's interpretation; outer appearance is merely the package in which inner reality lies hidden. Claustrophobic narrowness, no longer fragmented, brittle and reflected in mirrors, as in the bottomless uncertainty of *Despair,* is now a subconscious prison of repression, a pressurized cabin. Set designs are social definitions—the luxurious Wilhelmian apartments of Eva, the "high class whore," and the modernistic office of Pumms, the underworld boss. But isn't this a little too posterlike, too decorative? Don't the editing and cinematography conspire too obviously to bring these things to our attention?

When I think about the insistent subtlety with which Joseph Losey, for example, (or earlier, Renoir and Ophuls) whispered specifications for the sets, spacing, perspective and details in his best films, I sometimes get the impression with Fassbinder of roaring interruptions.

Here, the handling of the camera produces a flowing, quiet, distanced style, only occasionally broken into by disturbing closeups. However, while much of the cinematography, especially in the sequences in Biberkopf's living room (why do we see typesetting paraphernalia here?), only ventures a ritual movement within the room, the second central location in the story, Biberkopf's favorite pub—his "public domain" as opposed to the intimate "private sphere" of his rented room—remains flat and undeveloped, merely "surveyed." On one hand, we see Fassbinder's disciplined, elegant, finely measured defining of space, while on the other, he emphatically neglects these considerations. Is this his television dramaturgy?

Moments of weakness such as these can't be written off as the fault of Xaver Schwarzenberger. Even if we didn't know it as a fact, a certain amount of practical knowledge would make it evident that Fassbinder, who has declared that he only wants to work together with his new cameraman, actually had the final word on the editing and photography.

However, both director and cinematographer wished to pay homage to Sternberg. The varying usage of light inside rooms, the preference for "dim lighting and blackish-brown tones," the addition of a filter, which (as opposed to the hard, clear color contrasts in *Year of 13 Moons* and *Third Generation*, but already foreshadowed in the handling of color in *Despair)* produces a dulled softened light, can all be understood as a tribute to the director of *The Scarlet Empress, Shanghai Express* and *The Blue Angel*. It was *he* who developed this subtle use of lighting in his highly synthetic cinema. His graduated palette of light and shadow, with its subtly changing tonal impressions, allowed black-and-white films to convey a higher level of abstraction than is possible with color—unless color is handled expressionistically, as in Visconti's *Gotterdammerung*. Whether Sternberg's results can be achieved through the use of a filter, which tends to make everything look like watercolor, remains to be seen.

In any case, the technical aspects of the decor often seem to me to be the least successful, least original element in Fassbinder's *Alexanderplatz*. In this respect, he falls behind his work in such more compact masterworks as *In a Year of 13 Moons* and *The Third Generation*.

The less visible qualities—the stupendous intensity of Fassbinder's vision of Doblin, the emotional undertow which emanates from the numerous high points and depths in the narrative, brought together at the end in a grandiose partly unsuccessful, it seems to me, dream fresco—derive their power from the script and the actors.

Biberkopf, as portrayed by Gunther Lamprecht, is many people: the coward, the lustful animal, the sufferer, the bumbling fool, the bigmouth, the follower and blockhead, the good comrade and raging petty bourgeois, the beggar, the boozer and the lover—sensitive and vulnerable, arrogant and brutal. He is the poet who talks to his "little beer" the way Chaplin dances with his bread and fork, who dreams of a narrow middle-class life, who defends himself ferociously, tooth and nail. We witness how he sees Mieze for the first time, how he gives, or doesn't give, her flowers, how he gets drunk with her, how lonely he is, and how he learns about her death... Think about it: is it really possible to do all this with just one face, one heavy body and with just one arm? It's possible if your name is Gunther Lamprecht.

Then, there's Reinhold, played by Gottfried John—a stammering human enigma living a borrowed life—anxious and aggressive, servile and treacherous—but he cries when he encounters Franz, whose "most beloved in all the world" he has murdered.

Barbara Sukowa, certainly the greatest revelation in the film, is Mieze, the "innocent from the country", the "clean cut girl" (both quotes from Doblin), the naivete of the flesh. How does this young actress succeed (is it only the right eyebrows? the mouth? the voice? the way she says her lines? her use of dialect?)—how does she succeed in keeping this most emphatic love-image of Doblin's free from the cloying sweetness of kitsch? Incredibly, we don't *know* how. These are human beings, not prototypes or walking slogans. The affection with which Fassbinder extols the characters in Doblin's novel is his own. The women who cross Biberkopf's path, who stay with him for a while and then disappear, his friends and acquaintances, all have their mystery: they are living human beings. Hasn't Fassbinder gathered around him here nearly everyone with whom he has ever worked and lived? (Ingrid Caven and Kurt Raab are missing.) Living relationships. The sum.

Fassbinder tells the "story of Franz Biberkopf" as if Doblin had written it especially for him. He tells it from A to Z, faithful to the letter. Small additions are included: Fassbinder gives Doblin's orphaned Biberkopf a landlady, Frau Bast, who acts as a mother to him, and the landlord who gives him fatherly encouragement in the book is sketched more forcefully in the film. And where Doblin allows Franz to "mature," to peel off his childlike, good-natured "skin," in order to become humble, docile, unimportant—one among many—Fassbinder goes along, showing us through the dreams and the fantasies, the visions of dread, the tortures of guilt, his "purgatory." But where the salvation-seeking Doblin cries, "saved, judged, redeemed!" I hear Fassbinder (who perpetuates himself in the dream fresco as an Old Master with a slouch hat, dark glasses and a burning cigarette) whispering to himself, "definitely lost, finished."

At the root of the fears that burn Franz out, that were a source of suffering for him all his life, lie his own unacknowledged desires, unclear yearnings—his unfulfilled utopia. "And most deeply he loves two people: one is Mieze, with whom he's in love, and the other is—Reinhold." Fassbinder quotes this enigmatic, unfathomable sentence from the novel repeatedly in his film. That would have made Franz happy. Now, he's "tranquillized" (as it's put in the language of chemopsychiatry).

In the requiem he dedicates to Franz (My Dream of the Dream of Franz Biberkopf), Fassbinder outdoes himself. Never has he created a work so outrageous, so daring, so close to Pasolini (whose Biberkopf might have been named Accattone and whose hell is called Salo).

What story is Fassbinder finally telling us? The story of himself. Never has a filmic adaptation of a novel been so autobiographical. "There is not often such a noble bond between two such singular spirits." (Jean-Paul, Siebenkas.)

Annotated Filmography

By Wilhelm Roth

Synopses to films are useful: they refresh the memory; they help in identifying the films. For that reason, each of the following texts on Fassbinder's films will begin with a summary of the plot. Besides this, there are several other things to be considered: in many films, above all in the early gangster films, the stories cannot plausibly be told in a linear fashion—they must, rather, be often deduced from small hints. Combined in a text of a few lines, they obtain an unequivocal meaning they don't have in the film. Fassbinder's films, particularly the early ones, are films out of second hand, montage out of quotes. Even the plot details are to some extent prefabricated sets. Therefore, synopses don't tell much about the specific appeal of these films; although Fassbinder always tells stories in his films, here gestures and speech patterns are more important than reportable content. This is especially true of *Katzelmacher* and *Beware of a Holy Whore,* the two films about groups. With these, synopses are totally unproductive. The more Fassbinder's films become involved with reality, the more meaningful a synopsis becomes *(Merchant of the Four Seasons, Fear Eats the Soul).* One film is almost identical with its story, which has the greatest tempo; it can only be told: *Martha.*
W. R.

Der Stadtstreicher (1965)

Wandering through Munich, a man finds a pistol in an alley. He tries to get rid of the weapon, in vain. Two men who have been watching him for a while finally take the gun away from him.

In this film, which was shot in autumn, Munich becomes a "land of the soul." The bleakness of the city and the discovery of the pistol induce fantasies of suicide in the lonely man. *Stadtstreicher* can be seen as Fassbinder's response to his then favorite film, *Le Signe du Lion* by Eric Rohmer. Rohmer's film concerns a tramp who is going rapidly to seed in an almost empty Paris during the high summer holidays until he finally comes into an unexpected inheritance. While there is development in the Rohmer film, Fassbinder gives us only a snapshot. The before and after are left to the spectator's imagination.

Das Kleine Chaos (1966)

Three young people (Marite Greisele, Christoph Roser, Fassbinder) sell subscriptions to magazines door-to-door. They use this opportunity to be able to get into homes without being suspected to hold up a woman (Greta Rehfeld). They take her money and disappear without getting caught.

In *Kleine Chaos* Fassbinder's fascination with the American cinema is perceptible for the first time. The gestures and actions of the three mini-gangsters are based on Hollywood models. Fassbinder alters the schema, of course, in terms of content. In this film he fulfilled a desire, as he once put it, "to see a crime turn out well."

Love Is Colder than Death (1969)

Franz (Fassbinder), a small-time pimp, refuses to cooperate with a crime syndicate. The syndicate seems to give in, but sends the handsome Bruno (Ulli Lommel) to work on him. Franz loves Bruno. Bruno, whom the police don't know, commits a murder for which Franz becomes a suspect. However, the Commissioner (Yaak Karsunke) has no evidence against Franz. Eventually, Bruno and Franz decide to rob a bank. Joanna (Hanna Schygulla), Franz's girlfriend, betrays them to the police. Bruno has ordered a hit man from the syndicate to shoot Joanna during the confusion of the robbery. All plans fail. Bruno is shot by the police, but Franz and Joanna manage to flee.

Fassbinder's first feature film is obviously influenced by models, not all of which were introduced into the film by

Love Is Colder than Death

Fassbinder: Ulli Lommel chose a hat that was identical to one worn by Alain Delon in Melville's *Ice-Cold Angel*. Fassbinder was not familiar with Melville's films at the time. The general predeliction for gangster films, the suburban backdrop, the insistent peering of the camera, which recalls Straub, all reflect influences and ideas which were important to Fassbinder and the anti-teater team at the time. The travelling shot along Landsberger Strasse in Munich, in which we see solitary prostitutes standing around, is a variation on a shot from Straub's *The Bridegroom, the Actress and the Pimp.*

Despite all these influences and quotes, this is still a personal film which differs from two other Munich gangster films made at the time, Lemke's *48 Hours to Acapulco* and Thome's *Detective;* it is much shabbier, more desolate, farther removed from Hollywood. Fassbinder himself said in 1969, "What remains, when you have seen this film, is not that somebody killed six people, that a few murders happened, but that here are poor people, who can't get started, who have been put down, and for whom nothing is possible—who go farther than we would ever want to go—who have nothing, absolutely no opportunities." *(Film* 8/1969, p. 20) Franz, Bruno and Joanna are people who want affection and love, but who can only articulate this in helpless ways (as when Joanna informs the police about the robbery). They use gestures from gangster films because they have no language of their own.

In *Love Is Colder than Death,* there occur, almost like interludes, moments of comedy. In a supermarket Bruno and Joanna rip off delicacies in single shot of balletic elegance that goes on for a good four minutes: two movements (that of the two with the shopping cart and that of the camera) interweave, approach each other, separate again, to the accompaniment of a continually repeated, electronically distanced passage from Richard Straus' *Der Rosenkavalier.* In another scene (with obviously terroristic undertones), Bruno, Franz and Joanna, acting as if they didn't know one another, confuse a woman selling eyeglasses in a department store with so many questions, complaints and insults that they ultimately succeed in stealing three pairs of sunglasses. This type of comedy sequence can be found occasionally in other Fassbinder films: when Herr R wants to buy a phonograph record, he can't remember the title, so he tries to sing the melody, totally off-key, of course; especially in *Rio das Mortes* when Michel and Gunther expound their crazy ideas about growing cotton and raising sheep in Peru. Basically, though, Fassbinder's films are humorless. This has to do with the fact that they are so hermetically complete in themselves. Even if they are sometimes comic, they provoke a laughter that is more pained than liberating.

Katzelmacher (1969)

We meet four couples of varying stability: "Marie (Hanna Schygulla) belongs to Erich (Hans Hirschmuller); Paul (Rudolf Waldemar Brem) sleeps with Helga (Lilith Ungerer); Peter (Peter Moland) lets Elisabeth (Irm Hermann) support him, and Rosy (Elga Sorbas) does it with Franz (Harry Baer) for money."[1] This system of unstable equilibrium and chang-

Katzelmacher

ing relationships is thrown into disorder when an immigrant worker, Jorgos (Fassbinder), a "Greek from Greece," arrives and rents a room from Elisabeth. "Instinctive" dislike for the foreigner and sexual jealousy of the supposed potency of southern Europeans unites the group, with the exception of Marie, who "dates" Jorgos. The four men beat him up one day, hoping "to put him in his place." But Elisabeth, who is overcharging him, wants to keep him as a tenant. Helga and Paul decide to get married because she's pregnant, but then break up. Erich goes into the army, because "It's better than working." The future for Jorgos and Marie remains a question.

Katzelmacher is based on a play by the same title produced by Fassbinder for *anti-teater* in 1968. The play, which was only about 20 minutes long, is exclusively devoted to the Greek, the "Katzelmacher."[2] The first third of the film, before the arrival of the foreigner, is missing from the play. The characters stroll through the village square, in everchanging groups, encircling the foreigner, lunging at him, pulling back. The choreography is as important as the dialogue.

115

The film, which I saw for the first time in 1969, seemed lifeless and abstract compared to the play. The movements on the stage are replaced with a more rigid arrangement. There is less playing space, always shot in the same settings: a railing in front of a house, upon which the characters arrange themselves in various groupings; a table in a tavern; a backyard; several little rooms; all similar and scantily furnished. The milieu is no longer a village, but a suburb, perhaps Giesing. The characters deliver sentences, cartoonlike speech bubbles, quotables (in *Katzelmacher,* the so-called "Fassbinder-talk" is so unalloyed that it approaches self-parody). "Out of all this, there results an almost territorial domination of deadening recitations and of settings over the characters," (Peter W. Jansen, *Frankfurter Rundschau,* Oct. 4, 1969), whereas on the (setless) stage, the setting was identical with the movements of the characters.

At that time, I agreed very much with Wim Wenders' opinion: "The gruesome thing about this film is that down to the smallest detail, it is lifeless. Each change of scene is like an ill-tempered transition from the first to the second feature on a Saturday night, when each new change in the program makes us angrier and more unhappy. The fact that all the actors look so grim is not because they live in the provinces, which they represent, but because of the grim system, in which they are only marionettes, or at best, characters in a photo-novel, but even then with black bands over their eyes, like people in magazine photos who don't want to be recognized—'You'll never hear a word of tenderness from him,' as someone says in the film. In this death-film, only Hanna Schygulla is alive, so that we seem to see her in color." *(Filmkritik* 12/69, p. 751 ff.)

When I saw *Katzelmacher* again in 1974, the memory of the stage production had dimmed, and in spite of myself, I found the film much more lifelike than I had five years before. What I now feel coming from the film is an incredible rage. These so coldly and unlovingly depicted characters are really striking out with their helpless way of speaking, with their blows, as if they don't know what else to do, against the limits (of their consciousness and their self-consciousness). In both the play and the film, a fuse is always being lit, but the charge never goes off, and the film never explodes at any point. Even when the men gang up on the Greek there is no release; not in the context of the story, and still less for the spectator. The cold rage that the film gives off is a result of this.

People are dependent on each other and exploit this dependency; love collapses into exploitation; everything is buyable and whoever has the money can do anything (or almost anything); people will join forces against a stranger and finally leave him alone when they can take advantage of him (later a theme in *Fear Eats the Soul):* these are insights that have never been so aggressively formulated in a German film. However, doubts remain about the effectiveness of the film, because these insights are put forth as paradigms, not as real-life experience. If we compare Emmi and Ali in *Fear Eats the Soul*—a more humanly, differently depicted couple—we can see very clearly how Fassbinder has developed as a storyteller who wants to stimulate reflection.

I have a suspicion that the relative popularity of *Katzelmacher,* especially in northern Germany, is due above all to the curious synthetic Bavarian spoken by the characters: "Love and all that, that always has to do with money"; "He has money. And where there's money, you can do everything"; "Where he comes from, there's Communists"; "A Communist, that one, and justly forbidden." [3]

1. ARD (Syndicate of German Networks) brochure, Fiction Films on German Television, 1973, p. 55.
2. Bavarian expression: derogatory work for southern European immigrant workers. Popular etymology: Southerner who makes children with German women abundantly and simply (like cats). Correct etymology: Symbol for producers of wooden spoons (Gatzeln).
3. This is a loose translation of an ideosyncratic combination of German slang and Bavarian dialect which has no grammatical equivalent in English. (-trans.)

Gods of the Plague (1969)

Franz Walsch (Harry Baer) is let out of jail. He goes to his one-time girlfriend Joanna (Hanna Schygulla), who sings in a

Gods of the Plague

nightclub. He looks for his brother Marian (Marian Seidowski), and finds his dead body. Gunther (Gunther Kaufmann),
also known as Gorilla, confesses that he shot Marian:
"Marian sang... it was an order." In the meantime, Franz
has gotten to know Margarethe (Margarethe von Trotta) and
has left Joanna. Gunther, Franz and Joe, an older gangster
who lives in the country, plan to rob a supermarket. They are
betrayed by Joanna, who does ii because of her unrequited
love for Franz. But Margarethe also betrays them, out of
love for Franz. During the robbery, Franz and the manager
of the supermarket (Hannes Gromball) are shot. Gorilla
escapes and shoots the porn dealer (Carla Aulalu) whom
Joanna told about the robbery.

Gods of the Plague is in many ways a sequel to *Love Is
Colder than Death*. Harry Baer plays the role of Franz this
time (Fassbinder himself appears in a small cameo role). At
one point it is mentioned that Bruno is dead. Gunther, who
shot Marian, acted on orders (from the syndicate?). Joanna,
who has already betrayed Franz once out of love, now informs on him because he doesn't love her. And Joanna's

GÖTTE
DER
PEST

Ein Film
Rainer Wer
Fassbi

alph
film

Gods of the Plague

betrayal in the first film is now repeated by Margarethe for the same reason. As in the previous film, here, also, there is only one moment of absolute happiness for Franz—when he meets Gunther again, when they embrace and he exclaims "Crazy!". This responds to the certainly more coolly depicted reunion between Franz and Bruno. Both relationships are subject to strain: Bruno comes to Franz as a spy, and Gunther has killed his brother. In spite of this it doesn't seem to diminish Franz's feeling for them.

For me, this is the most personal of Fassbinder's early films, but also the most pessimistic, the darkest. The sets (the first used by Fassbinder in a film and especially built for it) are almost drowned in darkness; in this sunless Munich, petty gangsters and penniless women must meet with failure. Whether Margarethe loves Franz, or Joanna doesn't love him any more, the result is still the same. The characters are so very much alone, so little capable of opening up to one another, so isolated from history and society, that only loneliness or death can come to them in the end.

Fassbinder has integrated images from Hollywood and

French gangster films more forcefully into his vision here than in *Love Is Colder than Death*. These quotations are no longer (as with Lommel's Delon imitation) independent of the context, but are wholly integrated into the mythic, self-contained world of *Gods of the Plague*. A year later, these quotes and themes will be further elaborated upon in *The American Soldier*, almost like a Fassbinder gag-festival.

Why Does Herr R Run Amok? (1969)

The daily routine of an ordinary family: Herr Raab (Kurt Raab) is a technical designer, his wife (Lilith Underer) tends the house and their only child, a little boy (Amadeus Fengler). In the evening, the couple watch television, and on weekends they go for strolls or chat with Kurt's parents (Mr. and Mrs. Sterr). But this life has its small flaws: Herr R's hoped-for promotion on the job is a long time coming; his son is having trouble at school; the doctor finds some (of course insignificant) problems with Herr R's health, and, in general, Raab, who suffers from headaches, often functions rather absentmindedly. Only when a former friend from school (Peer Raben) comes to visit, does he liven up— together they sing the hymns they learned as children. Finally, Raab kills his wife, his son, and a neighbor (Irm Hermann) who has just dropped by, with a heavy lamp. The next morning he hangs himself in the toilet at the office.

This is a bad film, totally humdrum. The dialogue, improvised by the actors (Fassbinder and Fengler only sketched the outlines of the scenes), is of such banal ordinariness that it is almost painful to the listener. The film is already unbearable without its ending, and the washed-out colors contribute to the overall depressing atmosphere. We become aware of how abnormal the seemingly so normal daily routine of middle class existence really is.

Fassbinder and Fengler are not looking for anyone to blame here; neither the society nor the individual characters are held responsible for the disaster which ensues. Obvious mechanisms of repression are certainly evident—Raab's petty bourgeois background (his wife is his social "better"); his

boarding-school upbringing; his lack of recognition in his job. "Some insights appear like fat headlines, or, more seriously, like announcements in a police bulletin." (Alf Brustellin, *Suddeutsche Zeitung*, Feb. 2, 1971) What makes the film so desolate is not only its plot, but also its aesthetic approach. The stylization of the other films, the artificiality of the language, the ritualization of the actors' gestures, is transformed in *Herr R* (which does not "look like" a Fassbinder film) into a fetishization of real life. The actors, as well as they improvise, accomplish nothing more than a doubling of reality. Each scene lasts as long as it would in real life. If ever there was a naturalistic film, this is it. It lacks any utopian element, any notion of how a dignified life could be.

Rio das Mortes (1970)

Two friends, Michel (Michael Konig) and Gunther (Gunther Kaufmann) have a map of Peru, on which a treasure is indicated in the region of the Rio das Mortes. Despite the objections of Hanna (Hanna Schygulla), whom Michel wants to marry, the friends plan a trip to Peru. Their attempts to raise the money come to nothing until they find a rich patron (Hanna Axmann-Rezzori) who is fascinated by the treasure map and lends them the money. When Hanna fails to prevent the two from leaving, she aims a pistol at them as they are about to board the plane, but puts the weapon down again: an auto has driven into her line of sight.

Rio das Mortes is the funniest of Fassbinder's films. Many scenes—when Gunther and Michel try to raise money, when they investigate the situation in Peru, when they calculate their profits from sheep farming and cotton growing—acquire a bizarre humor because of the contrast between real conditions and the men's naive illusions. This contrast can only be reconciled in dream. The (in any case for the moment liberating) fairy-tale ending is only possible because the characters are more strongly anchored in reality than in the gangster films. They are not abandoned by Fate—the comedy acts as fairy-tale wish fulfilment to prevent it. Michael is a pipefitter; Gunther is a "child of the U. S. Occupation"—a Bavarian-speaking black who has just gotten out of the Bundeswehr, which he joined voluntarily to prove he is a "good German"; Hanna just wants to be a housewife and mother. The reason why she doesn't shoot them at the end, according to Fassbinder, is not simply because the auto got in the way: "If this were a film like the others I've made, she would have shot them, and then she would have taken it as seriously as, in fact, she does." *(Fernsehen und Film,* 2/1971, p. 43) *Rio das Mortes* also contains an (unusual for Fassbinder) insertion of cinema-verite: Michel, suddenly very well-informed about conditions in South America, interviews Carl Amory about the role of the Church in the political situation there.

The characters in this film are not trapped in a system like those in the gangster films or in *Herr R.* The film is more open, not determined by a single mood. That is in its favor, even if, compared to the stylistic closures of the other works, it is actually a smaller film.

Whity (1970)

The time is 1878, somewhere in the western part of the United States. In a mausoleum-like mansion lives the Nicholson family: the landowner Ben Nicholson (Ron Randall), his nymphomaniacally-inclined second wife Katherine (Katrin Schaake), and two sons from his first marriage, the homosexual Frank (Ulli Lommel) and the madman Davy (Harry Baer). Their obsequious mulatto servant, Whity (Gunther Kaufmann), is actually an illegitimate son of Ben's. Whity first acquires self-awareness when one after the other, the family members ask his help in killing other members of the family. Whity carries out the sentence that the Nicholsons long ago pronounced on one another: he shoots them all—Ben, Katherine, Frank and Davy—and leaves the small town with Hanna (Hanna Schygulla), a prostitute and saloon singer. In the desert they run out of water and die of thirst.

Whity was without doubt Fassbinder's least successful film. Its world premiere at the Berlin Film Festival in 1971

Rio das Mortes

found little understanding; it remains without a distributor, and has yet to be seen on television. The reasons are easy to see. The previous films all appeared to have, or at least they were so interpreted, something to say about German society, even if it was stated indirectly. With *Whity,* Fassbinder paid unqualified homage to Hollywood, and more, to Hollywood's most despised genre, the melodrama. As the critic Alf Brustellin wrote at the time, *Whity* cut a rather comic figure for this reason at the Berlin competition, "because almost any film that might have influenced this one never won a prize in any festival." *(Suddeutsche Zeitung,* July 8, 1971)

Even looking at it today, *Whity* is no great film. Nevertheless, it was important in Fassbinder's career, because it shows the beginnings of what would later become evident in *Beware of a Holy Whore*—a new, more professional, freer association with the medium of film. With this, there is also a loss: the unmediated way of seeing which nourished the suburban films, despite all their quotations, is missing here. *Whity* is the expression "of a, by this time, completely secondary experience." (Brustellin) Therefore, it would be unproductive to analyze the meaning of the content of *Whity*. The Nicholson dynasty stands for nothing but itself. Betrayal and murder, decadence and disintegration, are important only as colors and forms out of which the film is put together. *Whity* is almost like an etude, an attempt to make a film for a large public, in which a knowledge of cinema is connected to the visual experience of the audience. That this attempt fails (a re-make of the film would really be fascinating) has no doubt to do with the fact that *Whity* is still burdened down with too much of the *anti-teater* monotony.

Even if *Whity* is seen only as an exercise, it is still quite illuminating to study how Fassbinder has re-interpreted his influences. *Whity* reminds me, in its theme, of two films— Raoul Walsh's *Band of Angels* (1957) and von Sternberg's *Morocco* (1930). The Walsh film is about a plantation owner and former slaveholder (Clark Gable) who gives a good education to a young black (Sidney Poitier), who later, together with a half-caste girl, saves Gable's life in the Civil War. In *Morocco*, the cabaret singer (Marlene Dietrich) prefers a simple soldier (Gary Cooper), as Hanna does the black man Whity. Marlene gives Cooper an apple (and the key to her room) and Hanna presents Whity with a rose. Both couples head for the desert at the end, where privation certainly awaits Cooper and Marlene, but not death. Characteristically, Fassbinder refuses a happy ending to the stories he has appropriated. *Whity* is a film of pessimism. When Whity and Hanna dance together in the desert before they die of thirst, it is a defiant gesture that does not cancel the pessimism.

Whity is the first of Fassbinder's films to be shot by Michael Ballhaus, who has also done the camerawork on *Beware of a Holy Whore, The Bitter Tears of Petra von Kant, Welt am Draht* and *Martha*. In his other films, Fassbinder worked with Dietrich Lohmann and eventually, Jurgen Jurges. I don't think his choice of a cameraperson is ever by chance. Ballhaus has done the "rich" films (with the exception of *Petra*, which only cost about 325,000 DM), and Lohmann and Jurges the "poor" ones. All the Ballhaus films are in color. His lighting is different from theirs. In "his" films, the characters don't emerge out of the darkness in

Whity

order to disappear back into it. His light is uniform, and
never draws attention to itself, always to the story. Fassbinder seems to have engaged Ballhaus exclusively for films
which disengage themselves from descriptions of everyday
reality, and which create their own narrative-reality. Ballhaus
has photographed all of Fassbinder's films which are closest
to Hollywood; *Martha* is their collaborative masterpiece.

Fassbinder is the only young film director in the Bundesrepublik who has been able to work continually for the past
five years. As a result of his frequently-belittled diligence and
almost hectic overproduction, none of Fassbinder's films appeared to have a claim to any meaning beyond that of the
moment *(Effi Briest* seems to have changed that). Since the
acquisition of money was really not a problem for Fassbinder, he could afford to carry out projects like *Whity*—
680,000 DM for an experiment that failed (if we judge the
success of a film by whether or not it reaches the public). He
could afford to make mistakes because not every film had to
be made to assimilate the ideas, dreams and frustrations of
five years into one good piece of work, as would be the case

with Haro Senft, to take an extreme example. If Fassbinder's 1973-74 films like *Martha, Fear Eats the Soul* and *Effi Briest* were successful, it is certainly not least of all for the very reason that he was able to try out the things that interested him, even if, in doing so, he occasionally failed.

Die Niklashauser Fart (1970)

In a timeless epoch, which outwardly most resembles today's Europe, but also in part, the Third World, as well as the European Middle Ages and Rococo period, a shepherd (Michael Konig) appears as a lay preacher. He is accompanied by several followers, the most influential of whom is the Black Monk, a young man in a black leather jacket (Fassbinder). The preacher maintains that "the Virgin Mary has given me a sign," and soon begins to raise revolutionary demands in his sermons. He comes into conflict with the Church, but finds followers among the poor peasants. He also arouses the interest of Margarethe, a wealthy woman (Margit Carstensen). However, his followers mistake his revolutionary exhortations for religious prophecies, and for Margarethe, religious zeal is mixed with sexual attraction. After an informer reports them to the Bishop, the preacher is apprehended by two German policemen and two American MPs, and a massacre ensues. The preacher and three followers are crucified in an automobile graveyard. An insurrection breaks out, after which we hear the words of the Black Monk: "But he and his comrades had learned from their mistakes. They went to the mountains, and three years later, the revolution was victorious."

The plot of the film is based on a historical incident: on March 24, 1476, in the free city of Niklashauser, Hans Bohm, a shepherd, declared that the Mother of God had appeared to him. He raised concrete revolutionary demands and for a time gathered 30,000 disciples in Niklashauser; they considered him a new Messiah and waited for a miracle. Bohm was arrested by the Bishop's army and was burned at the stake on July 15, 1476.

Originally, Fassbinder had merely wanted to tell this story

in a linear fashion, but eventually came to the decision that "we should really tell something that has to do with us. Isn't that much more important than the story of this Hans Bohm?" (Fassbinder and Fengler, *Television Plays on West German Networks,* July-Dec., 1970, p. 43) For this reason, Fassbinder dealt freely with costumes and historical periods, and allowed his characters to speak the language of the 15th Century, but also, for example, to cite quotations from Camillo Torres. A black man reads aloud a report of the assassination of a Black Panther leader from a newspaper, and slogans from the student movement ("Destroy what destroys you!") are quoted, because "The audience shouldn't begin thinking, 'Oh yeah, that was 1496.' That thought would reassure them, but they should be disturbed." (Fassbinder and Fengler, op. cit., p. 42)

The film should "show how and why a revolution fails," and Fassbinder's answer is that it did not result in a better future because the people had lost sight of the proper consciousness: "It is part of their wretched condition that they can't conceive of anything at all different." (op. cit., p. 42) Here, he has also come to a decision about the political function of art, because in this film it is really a question of to what extent one "can use dramatic methods to convey radical insights, and consequently, whether one can make films or whatever with this objective. We came to the conclusion that it is not a matter of going into the mountains—for God's sake, please!—or of imagining other possibilities." (Fassbinder in an interview, Feb. 20, 1974)

In order to characterize the false consciousness of his hero, Fassbinder styles the action after the model of Christ's Passion: the shepherd becomes a Christ-figure, and Margarethe, the Mary Magdalene. References to political reality (past and present) are ranged alongside quotations from Christian legends and other films. In this respect, Fassbinder has addressed himself to many of the themes dealt with in Godard's *Weekend.* Both films feature long dialogues, the appearance of bizarrely dressed revolutionary groups on the edge of the woods, and sudden manifestations of people from other centuries, including an armed follower of Hans Bohm who is modelled upon the title character in Glauber Rocha's *An-*

tonio das Mortes. However, such influences function in *Niklashauser Fahrt* more clearly than in any of Fassbinder's other films, as the components of a collage: their origin in other contexts remains intentionally recognizable. References to foreign films are, so to speak, pieces of cultural debris, like old church chorales—or bids to the discerning consciousness of the spectator, as are the political slogans quoted by characters in the film.

Otherwise, as with Godard, the discussions in *Niklashauser Fart* offer nothing new, but because of frequent repetition, dramatically similar scenes have a rather monotonous effect. (That we don't get this impression in *Katzelmacher* is due to the fact that in each scene, concrete changes in concrete situations can be perceived, while the discussion scenes in *Niklashauser Fart* are invariably abstract.) In this film, three excellent sequences stay in the memory: the Bishop sniffs at a peasant in order to savor the odor of work; an aerial shot shows how, as the shepherd preaches in a quarry, his words echo back off the walls—a striking image of his isolation; finally, the scene in which Hanna Schygulla rehearses a political text in front of a mirror while Fassbinder directs her in the background—an abrupt incursion of reality into the otherwise rather abstract continuity of the film.

The way in which Fassbinder incorporates his reflections on the political function of art into the medium of film makes *Niklashauser* a special case, not only in his work, but in the new German cinema. A key experience of Fassbinder's generation, the failure of the political protest movement, especially obvious in Paris in 1968, has not been dealt with so radically anywhere else in German cinema.

P.S.: There is only one known print of *Niklashauser Fart,* which can be found in the archives of the Westdeutscher Rundfunk in Cologne. This copy is so damaged that it is unfit for public screening. Through the friendly cooperation of the WDR, I was able to inspect the film on the editing machine on March 16, 1974.

The American Soldier (1970)

Three Munich policemen (Jan George, Hark Bohm, Marius Aicher) have hired the professional killer Ricky (Karl Scheydt), an American from Munich who has just returned from Vietnam. He has to bump off several people whom they, as agents of the law, cannot kill as easily. Before the dispatch of his first assignment Ricky runs into his old friend Franz Walsch (Fassbinder). Ricky's first victim is a gypsy (Ulli Lommel). Then he has to do away with Magdalena Fuller (Katrin Schaake), a woman who sells pornography and information; when her boyfriend arrives, he shoots him too. When Ricky calls for a prostitute in a hotel, the porter sends him Rosa von Praunheim (Elga Sorbas), the mistress of one of the policemen. She falls in love with Ricky. Ricky visits his mother (Eva Ingeborg Scholz) and his brother (Kurt Raab). Ricky's last assignment is to kill Rosa von Praunheim; he carries it out without hesitation. The final showdown occurs at the railroad station. Ricky and Franz are gunned down by the police because they were distracted by the unexpected arrival of Ricky's mother and brother. While the mother stands paralyzed with fear in the background, the brother throws himself upon Ricky's dead body. This final shot is a slow-motion sequence.

Among all the gangster films, *American Soldier's* influences are the most easily recognized: Ricky resembles Paul Muni in Hawks' *Scarface;* there is also the well-known Hawksian incestuous relationship between brothers. Fassbinder also quotes himself—not just names, but a number of characters and situations. There is even a second-hand quote: Magdalena Fuller, the dealer in porn and information, is a character from *Gods of the Plague,* where she was called Carla and played by Carla Aulaulu. (The Magdalena Fuller in *Plague* was only a cameo role for Ingrid Caven.) This female dealer-character originated in a Fuller film, *Pickup on South Street* (1952), in which Thelma Ritter played the newspaper dealer Moe Williams, who worked part-time as a police informer.

In *American Soldier,* a number of dissociated elements are juxtaposed: quotations, episodes, stories. For example, Margarethe von Trotta, as the chambermaid, tells (as a kind of preview) the story of *Fear Eats the Soul,* even if with a different ending. Then she herself plays out a crazy story: she stabs herself in the chest with a dagger after her lover breaks up with her over the telephone. However, nobody pays any attention to her. Even the film forgets her immediately, as it does other episodes. If there weren't a certain melancholy-gloomy atmosphere to give the film unity (an ''artistic aura''—Frieda Grafe, *Suddeutsche Zeitung,* Dec. 7, 1970), it would break apart into its many details.

Beware of a Holy Whore (1970)

In a hotel somewhere on the Spanish coast, a film crew waits for the director, the star, the equipment, and the production money from Bonn. The mood swings from apathy to hysteria. When the director Jeff (Lou Castel) arrives with the star (Eddie Constantine as Eddie Constantine), he finds himself instantly surrounded by chaos. Couples and groups intermingle. Eddie, who is twenty years older than most of the

other members of the team, is as neglected as a fossil until he makes contact with Hanna (Hanna Schygulla). Meanwhile, preparations for the film move along. Jeff explains an especially complicated shot to the cameraman, and tells Eddie the basic idea of the film, *Patria o Meurte:* it will be a film "against state-sanctioned violence." The crew, who feel increasingly dependent on Jeff, rebel in small, senseless ways: Jeff has confrontations with all of them. Nevertheless, the shooting of the film finally commences.

Holy Whore is a key work in Fassbinder's career, an ending and also a beginning. It is the last film in which Fassbinder speaks more or less directly about his obsessions. The film marks the end of a collective which came together in the Action-Theater and *anti-teater,* and made up the crew in his earlier films. On the other hand, here Fassbinder shows a new, for him, interest in staging. What up to now he had only succeeded in doing in his best theatrical productions (above all in *Katzelmacher* and *The Coffee House),* he now does in film—demonstrating how people in groups are dependent on one another through exploitation and subjugation, sadism and masochism. The precise control of language and choreographic arrangements on the stage are consistent with the very complex editing and complicated but intelligible cinematography we see here. It is also evident in *Holy Whore* that something is ending and something new beginning, in the treatment of the duality in the character of Jeff: while he takes on the hysterical tone of the rest of the crew in all his personal confrontations with them, he explains his ideas to the cameraman calmly, masterfully, very much like a craftsman.

Holy Whore is a distanced recapitulation of the making of *Whity.* According to Fassbinder, it is also a film about what happened while *Holy Whore* was being made. Those familiar with the "Fassbinder clan" can easily name the real-life model for each of the characters in the film. In many cases Fassbinder hasn't gone to any trouble to conceal these models: Lou Castel, as Jeff, wears Fassbinder's black leather jacket from the earlier films; Irm, the woman Jeff sends away, is played by Magdalena Montezuma, but the voice is actually synced by Irm Hermann; Hanna Schygulla is named

Hanna in the film, too. She is self-assured, and, because of her strong ego, nicer than the other women in the film. In this, her character also corresponds to the images of women she has played in earlier films. However, this inside information is only relatively important; the film is understandable even without this special knowledge. *Beware of a Holy Whore* is the merciless self-representation of an artist. He sees himself as a kind of vampire who exploits all the members of a group, a crew, a collective, for his own ends, but also as a collector and coordinator who brings the talents of the others together, without which the film couldn't be made. His profession, making films, is for him a unique form of prostitution, in which everyone from the makeup woman to the director is included. The changing erotic relationships, which result not from affinity but from title of ownership, are the more direct expression of this prostitution. To make films means to carry out artificial actions, or, as Thomas Mann put it (which Fassbinder quotes at the end of the film), "I tell you that I am often deathly tired of representing the human without taking part in what is human..." (from *Tonio Kroger*).

Holy Whore functions as an act of liberation only because of this—certain things are perceived and declared. Also, from this point on, Fassbinder will work with a team that will alter very slowly, with the addition of new members, but the collective will be only a convenient form for film (and theatrical) work, not an ideology. Also from now on, Fassbinder will tell "his" stories, but they will be less determined by autobiographical elements, and he will see himself as a director who occasionally films other people's stories (Fleisser, Kroetz, Galouye, Ibsen, Fontane). Nevertheless, this foreign matter, in Fassbinder's hands, will pass through a process of metamorphosis through which it will be integrated into his own world.

Three remarks: according to the dialogue, the film takes place in Spain, but it was actually shot in Italy (Sorrento). Optical references to the location have not been deleted.—The young man with the long blond hair who tells the story of Goofy in the first scene is the filmmaker Werner Schroeter *(Eika Katappa, Salome, Willow Springs,* etc.)

—When Irm (played by Schroeter's favorite actress Magdalena Montezuma) departs, she travels over the sea by motorboat; a quote from *Eika Katappa.* Schroeter re-directed this sequence for Fassbinder. Here, the musical background is by Donizetti; in *Eika Katappa,* it was by Hugo Wolf.

Pioneers in Ingolstadt (1970)

When the Pioneers are stationed in Ingolstadt, the girls liven up. Each, according to her temperament and inclination, looks for a beau or a Great Love. While Alma (Irm Hermann) picks up passing soldiers, the serving maid Berta (Hanna Schygulla) falls in love with the initially shy Karl (Harry Baer). For him, she is only a passing fancy. He leaves her.

For me, this film is, along with *Nora Helmer,* Fassbinder's weakest work. In a film that is already confused, the setting and the atmosphere don't tally. Fassbinder wanted to bring references to the present into the story, which was written by Marieluise Fleisser during the Weimar period (1927) and originally set in the time of the Kaiser. So the girls wear miniskirts, and we see the sign of the anti-nuclear movement on a wall. Fabian Unertl (Rudolf Waldemar Brem) borrows a BMW from his father when he wants to seduce a girl, and one of the soldiers (Max, played by Gunther Kaufmann) is black. On the other hand, some of the uniforms are decorated with Nazi emblems. This confusion came about because the network (ZDF) would not allow the film to be made with modern German army uniforms.[1]

Whether Fassbinder's distortion of the relationship between Karl and Berta had to do with the bad circumstances under which he had to work is impossible to say. "The play has a more modest social logic: soldiers must be brutal, casual lovers because their profession makes them that way. The illusions of the chambermaid Berta are broken by this desolate reality. Her mistake was to believe abstractly and naively in the goodness of humanity. She is incapable of perceiving even the simplest social relationships. Fassbinder's film comes from a more expansive illogic, because he destroys precisely this social context through abstruse modifications and additions. The soldier Karl, played by Harry Baer, is now a weaker film hero, a character of vague melancholy, but not someone who guards himself against his (in any case hopeless) feelings by being brutal. Hanna Schygulla is the only one who brings the pace of Fleisser's small town to life in Fassbinder's motley world: she gives the little gestures of love such a very solemn importance that the story of a domestic servant becomes a great melodrama of painful love. At the end of the film, she rolls on the ground in a woodland glade, crying—here, Fassbinder's film turns into a tough-sentimental piece of work." (Benjamin Henrichs, *Fernsehen und Film,* 5/1971, p. 51)

1. In the Dresden premiere in 1928, the story took place after the war. After the Berlin production of the play in 1929, Herbert Jhering wrote, "In the Berlin production the story takes place before the war. Were they afraid of conflicts with the Reichswehr?" (Quoted in *Von Reinhardt bis Brecht,* Vol. 2, p. 393, Berlin, DDR, 1961.)

Merchant of the Four Seasons (1971)

Hans Epp (Hans Hirschmuller) joined the Foreign Legion in order to get away from the unloving domination of his mother (Gusti Kreissl). When he returns, she greets him by telling him, "The best ones stay abroad so that someone like you can come back." He joins the police force, but is soon dismissed when he allows himself to be seduced by a prostitute while on duty. He becomes a produce vendor, selling his wares in courtyards. His "great love" would not marry him because he was socially inferior to her. His wife (Irm Hermann) doesn't love him and only nags him. He pays frequent visits to bars to avoid her; at home, he strikes out at her in a helpless rage. When she decides to divorce him, he suffers a heart attack. He recovers and the couple remain together. Since Hans can't work hard any more, he hires an assistant, Anzell (Karl Scheydt), with whom his wife spent the night once while he was in the hospital. In order to get rid of her

Merchant of the Four Seasons

1972) What overwhelmed the critics and what is certain even troublesome ex-lover, she prevails upon him to sell the fruit for more than agreed upon with Hans. Eventually Hans catches him, as she knew he would, and fires him, but realizes that his wife has set a trap for him and Anzell. In a bar he meets Harry (Klaus Lowitsch), with whom he served in the Foreign Legion. Harry comes to work for him, and wins the confidence of his wife and little daughter (Andrea Schober), whom he helps with her homework. Hans becomes more and more silent; he senses that he is no longer needed. He makes a farewell visit to his family, and from there goes to his hangout where he systematically drinks himself to death in the presence of his wife, Harry, and others. After the funeral, the widow and Harry decide to team up.

No other Fassbinder film has received such uniformly favorable notices from the critics. Gunther Pflaum wrote, "As far as I am concerned, this is the best German film since the war." *(Suddeutsche Zeitung,* May 31, 1972) Wilfried Wiegand said, "This is one of the most important German films in years." *(Frankfurter Allgemeine Zeitung,* May 31,

Merchant of the Four Seasons

now is the simplicity with which Fassbinder tells his story, the
mastery with which he fills this traditional framework with
life by taking elements from countless trivial films, most of
them melodramas. "Fassbinder triumphs over these cliches
by making the emotions which they convey genuine." (Urs
Jenny, *Filmkritik* 5/72) He still deals with the most dreadful
characters—the mother, the wife—indulgently, almost with
affection. Behind their harshness, their vulnerability and
helplessness become apparent. The mother, head of one of
Fassbinder's fatherless families, wants to transform her son
into an ersatz-father. The wife is not loving, but then, she
doesn't get any love from her husband, who was already a
broken man when he married her.

Fassbinder's greatest sympathy, however, is reserved for
Hans; the film is made from his point of view. Even in the
few scenes in which he is not present (when his wife goes to
her mother-in-law for help; when she goes to bed with
Anzell; when she reaches an agreement with Harry after the
funeral), the characters behave as he might imagine they
would, as he fears, knows or foresees, as they must, in fact,

act in reaction to his reaction, which is in turn an answer to their reaction, etc. Against this vicious circle, which he initially tried to escape (he is the first Fassbinder hero who not only succeeds in fleeing, which also happens in *Rio das Mortes,* but who also comes back, disillusioned), he eventually offers no more resistance at all. His gradual descent into silence, a stronger indictment than any cry, however loud, gives the film its unusual emotional impact. Fassbinder conceived this family tragedy not only as a personal drama, but also in relation to the times in which is is set. *Merchant of the Four Seasons* is the first work in the new German cinema about the 1950s, the Adenauer era, the "economic miracle". The clothes and hair styles, the interior decoration and cuisine—depict very visually that narrowness from which there is no escape. There are anachronisms: many refer farther back, to the Nazi era—Hanna Schygulla's white dress and piled-up hair—and the names: Epp was a well-known Nazi from Bavaria, and the family lawyer is named von Schirach. Others are from the present: the automobile licenses and telephones. But while in *Pioneers in Ingolstadt* the agelessness created by bringing in historical references at random is confusing and annoying, here the breaks function as deliberate irritations. The story definitely takes place in the postwar period and has its roots there, but the things which made such a story possible have not yet been overcome.

1. The title is translated literally from the French, and sounds as strange in German as it does in English. In France, an itinerant fruit and vegetable vendor is called "marchand de quatre saisons."

The Bitter Tears of Petra von Kant *(1972)*

Petra von Kant (Margit Carstensen), a successful Bremen fashion designer, lives with her secretary Marlene (Irm Hermann) in a spacious apartment. Her first husband, by whom she has a daughter, Gabriele (Eva Mattes), was killed in an accident, and she is divorced from her second. She falls in love with a model, Karen Thimm (Hanna Schygulla), who is

The Bitter Tears of Petra Von Kant

a good ten years younger than she. Petra wishes to take total control over the young Karin: Karin uses the wealthy Petra, but wants to keep her own freedom. When Karin's husband, who was in Australia, suddenly returns, Karin goes back to him. Petra is despondent. Gradually, however, she begins to understand: "I never loved Karin at all—I only wanted to possess her." She offers Marlene, whom she has up to now treated like an object, collaboration, freedom and amusement, but the secretary, who never says a word, silently packs her bags and leaves.

The film was originally a theatre piece, which had its premiere at the Experimenta in Frankfurt in 1971, and was a critical failure. Fassbinder did not alter the action of the play when he filmed it: everything takes place in one apartment, almost exclusively in one room. The film is the study of a room, and of the woman who inhabits that room and puts her mark on everything contained therein, as does the camera. The room is quite playful, a bit trashy—half-1920's, half-modern. It is unthinkable that a man could live here.

When Karin appears, there is a moment of happiness. Here

are two women, disillusioned with men, emancipated: Petra, ambitious, cultivated, precise in her language, sensitive; Karin, lazy, ignorant, blunt and inexact in her speech. Opposites, therefore, but there is a possibility for happiness, as long as the past and the outside world are not allowed in. But that, of course, is impossible, and their love must fail.

Men, who are banished from this room, are constantly present in the attitudes of the two women. Petra and Karin play the old games of desire for domination and jealousy, oppression and dependency.

This is a film between art and kitsch, between good taste and sham (Petra is designing a collection for Karstadt!). And nevertheless, this melodrama must be taken seriously, as it takes itself seriously (the thin line separating it from self-parody is never crossed). When Petra, deserted by Karin, begins to rave and rant, her outburst (not least because of Carstensen's performance) has a power that sweeps away the possible objections of the audience. "Her commanding, mannered behavior, her supposed emancipation, the costly and lucid aloofness of her language, all this falls apart. She treads wildly in her silver sandals, tearfully shattering a tea service. Her friend, her mother, her daughter, stare in disbelief. There is more being destroyed here than an individual; 'culture' itself is falling apart. Without a doubt, Fassbinder is giving his version of *Death in Venice*." (Reinhard Baumgart, *Suddeutsch Zeitung*, Dec. 8, 1972) What looks like an affront to good taste simply invalidates standards of taste. "To feel so much, to suffer so much, to be as dependent as is this Petra von Kant, that is, precisely—tasteless. Consequently, the most extreme display of genuine feeling is manifested with an extreme of unnatural stylization." (op. cit.)

Jail Bait (1972)

Fourteen-year-old Hanni (Eva Mattes), who is treated like a helpless child by her middle-class parents (Jorg von Liebenfels, Ruth Drexel), meets Franz (Harry Baer), a nineteen-year-old worker, and sleeps with him. A jealous

Jail Bait

friend reports them to the authorities, and Franz is sentenced to nine months in jail for seducing a minor. After he is released early for good behavior, the couple meet again regularly, although they now attempt to remain unobserved. When Hanni gets pregnant, she persuades Franz to shoot her father, because he stands in the way of their love. The crime is discovered some time afterwards, and Franz is apprehended. Hanni visits him in jail and tells him that their child died at birth.

When the film was seen on television, there was a controversy over a closeup of a penis, which was deleted by the censors from the film version. The critics objected to it because they thought that Fassbinder had dealt with the characters, especially the parents, in a derogatory way. They found support in the protest of Franz Xaver Kroetz against this adaptation of his play. Kroetz objected not only to the scenes which Fassbinder added (the father assaults his daughter rather lustfully at one point; while her boyfriend is in jail, Hanni tries to pick up an immigrant worker), but described the film as altogether pornographic: ''I call the

Jail.Bait

denunciation of humanity which this film pursues obscene.
The girl is no pre-nymphomaniacal fly-by-night, she is only
trying to break away from the narrowmindedness of her
Catholic background, and at the same time experiences a
marvelous love story. And the boy is no sex fiend, but a love-
starved man." (Kroetz, *Munchner Abendzeitung*, Mar. 8,
1973) Fassbinder defended himself, saying, "Everything in
the film is also in the play." (Fassbinder, *Abendzeitung*,
Mar. 12, 1973) Kroetz won a lawsuit against Fassbinder, and
the passages which had offended him were removed from the
film.

Actually, Fassbinder's *Jail Bait* is in danger, at times, of
betraying its characters to visual effects and directorial agili-
ty. If, however, the film stays in balance in its best passages,
it is due to the dialogue in which it becomes obvious that the
parents have done nothing more than transfer the oppression
under which they themselves suffered as young people, to
their daughter. It is thanks to Ruth Drexel and Eva Mattes
especially, who bring something of the ambiguity of Kroetz's
characters into the now (compared with, say, *Merchant of*

the Four Seasons or *Fear Eats the Soul*) posterlike world of Fassbinder.

The real point of Fassbinder's re-working of the original (and the reason why Fassbinder was interested in it) is first discernible in the closing (not criticized by Kroetz) scene. Hanni says to Franz, "It wasn't true love. It was only physical." He agrees with her, but simultaneously lays his hand on her shoulder, and with this gesture, the most tender in the whole film, contradicts his words. He really loved Hanni. Indeed these two, Hanni and Franz, are victims of their petty bourgeois environment. However, while Kroetz's sympathy goes above all to Hanni, Fassbinder sympathizes primarily with the young man. It was already obvious earlier, after Franz was released, that Hanni had him in the palm of her hand, and because of this, in the legal sense, he again becomes the guilty party, although it was she, the more active of the two, who drove him to kill. But we only understand at the end of the film why Franz really committed murder: because he loved Hanni.

Jail Bait stands closer to the earlier suburban "gangster" films than to *Beware of a Holy Whore, Merchant of the Four Seasons* or *Petra von Kant,* not only because of its milieu, but also its "philosophy." A man will always be betrayed by the woman he loves.

Eight Hours Are Not a Day (1972)

Part 1. *Jochen and Marion.* Grandma Kruger (Luise Ullrich) lives in Cologne with her daughter Kathe, her son-in-law, and their son Jochen (Gottfried John). Among those who attend her 60th birthday party are her younger daughter, the spinsterish Klara, as well as Monika, Jochen's sister, who is unhappily married to Harald (Kurt Raab). When Jochen goes to fetch champagne from an automatic vending machine, he becomes acquainted by chance with Marion (Hanna Schygulla), and spontaneously invites her to accompany him to the party. Jochen is a tool maker in a large factory, where his work group has been promised an efficiency bonus. Marion works in the advertising department of the

Cologne City Advertiser with Irmgard Erlkonig, who has very conservative ideas, and is prejudiced against Marion's boyfriend because he's only a worker. Marion breaks with her former friend because of Jochen. In the park, Grandma strikes up a conversation with Gregor Mack (Werner Finck), a widowed pensioner, and the two become friends. Grandma makes up her mind to find an apartment of her own. Jochen's work group's bonus is cancelled, because in the opinion of the management, Jochen's proposal for reform made the pay increase excessive. The workers deliberately sabotage production. The company has to hold up its delivery schedule, and so submits to them and pays the increase. Kretschmer, the foreman, who came into conflict with the workers because of the sabotage, dies unexpectedly.

Part 2. *Grandma and Gregor.* Grandma and Gregor are looking for a place to live. Because of the excessive rents, Grandma wants to establish a housing agency for elderly people, but then puts another plan into action: she organizes a kindergarten in the vacant rooms of a former city library. Jochen's colleagues help with the equipment. The police close the kindergarten, but the neighborhood mothers succeed, with the help of the press and especially, with a children's demonstration, in getting the school reopened, now under the direction of a kindergarten teacher who, as is only fair, will be Grandma. Franz Miltenberger, a somewhat older work colleague of Jochen's, gets up the courage to apply for the job of foreman. The supervisor tells him, however, that the company doesn't want to hire the new foreman from its own staff.

Part 3. *Franz and Ernst.* The workers notify the supervisor that they want Franz as their foreman. Franz makes a miscalculation which seems, finally, to have deprived him of any chance of getting the job. The worker Rudiger, who has a strong prejudice against any kind of solidarity, informs on an innocent immigrant worker, Giuseppe. A new foreman arrives, but he is ignored at first, though he tries to gain the confidence of the workers. Soon it becomes apparent that he would actually rather have another position in the company, so that he doesn't stand in the way of Franz's application. He willingly helps Franz in his preparations for the test he must take for the foreman's job. Franz passes the test, and the supervisor kindly promises to recommend him to management.

Part 4. *Harald and Monika.* Marion's mother finds Jochen in bed with her daughter and throws him out. She is not at all pleased that he's only a worker. Harald forbids Monika to take a job outside the home. He wants to raise their daughter in an authoritarian way. Monika decides to get a divorce. Jochen and Marion get married. Manfred, Jochen's co-worker and best friend, begins to fall in love with Monika. At the wedding reception, Harald agrees to a divorce and Miss Erlkonig finally kisses a worker.

Part 5. *Irmgard and Rolf.* The company plans to transfer the toolmaking division to another part of Cologne, which causes many problems for the dismayed workers. Because of the transfer, Jochen wants to exchange his new apartment with that of his parents, but his father is initially vehemently against it. The workers suggest to the supervisor that they organize the pace of the work themselves. The supervisor refuses, but the director of the company agrees, and informs the workers that he's only doing it because it suits his own interests. Miss Erlkonig has fallen in love with a worker she met at the wedding. Monika has moved in with her parents. She had given over her savings to a questionable businessman who had advertised incredible profits from investments; Grandma intervenes to clear the matter up. Miss Erlkonig and her new lover move in with Marion and Jochen. In the apartment which Grandma shares with Gregor, Monika and Manfred declare their love.

This television series is directed to the widest possible audience, and for this reason, it greatly resembles conventional family series and shows typical identification figures who are based on models from popular theatre: the young lovers in secret alliance with crafty old folks; family events (birthdays, weddings, funerals) as rallying points for the action; surprises, mixups and humorously depicted misunderstandings. Nevertheless, Fassbinder's series diverges dramatically from this schema, in that, contrary to popular theatre (and classic comedy), what is lacking is a certain malicious glee about negative characters.

Additional tension is given to the series by an effectively handled elliptical narrative style, which again and again startles the spectator with facts which were foreshadowed in a preceding installment, but which he could not witness (as he had might have wanted to). These frequent moments of surprise and hindsight enliven the series, which was a great success with the television audience.

Fassbinder has smuggled more socio-political insights into *Eight Hours Are Not a Day* than have ever before been attempted in an entertainment film. Numerous problems which are important to most viewers in their everyday lives are touched upon and are, through the evasion of any didactic tones, clarified in all their psychological, social and political interconnections. For example, some of the problems dealt with are public transportation fares, high rents and the influence of real estate brokers, participation in management activities, antiauthoritarian education, prejudice against members of a lower social class (workers) and minorities (immigrant workers), possible self-initiatives for the politically least active groups in society (pensioners, housewives). The plot also illustrates certain ideas without calling them by abstract names. We learn, for instance, what a psychosomatic illness is (the death of the foreman); that misplaced gratification is rooted in frustration (Monika eats one sausage after another and declares, "Unsatisfied wives just eat more.") When Franz Miltenberger thinks he has lost any chance of becoming foreman, he gets drunk at the local pub and keeps mumbling "I'm dumb and I wanna stay dumb," we witness an outpouring of feeling. The basic concepts of alienation and surplus value are elucidated in everyday speech. Alienated work: "It's just work that has nothing to do with us..." (Marion, Part 2). Surplus value: "I see now that when we work, we only work part-time for ourselves..." (Marion, Part 5). Fassbinder made painstaking preparations for the series: "For *Eight Hours Are Not a Day* we researched the stories to see whether they were possible, because we always worked the stories out for ourselves first, and also many stories that were not in the film, and talked with trade unionists...we worked a whole year before the script was ready." (Interview, Feb. 20, 1974) The series received an unusually mixed reception from the critics. Rejection by conservative critics was unanimous, and many left and liberal critics were also vehement. Almost all the critics stated as their main argument that the series did not convey a realistic image of workers. As it was stated, for example, in the *Television and Network Mirror of the German Industrial Institute* (No. 17, Jan. 25, 1973), "As large a view of society as that of the workers is entitled to a realistic and representative depiction of their various problems." In the *Frankfurter Rundschau* (Dec. 16, 1972), Heiko R. Blum called the second part "a story full of naivete, departures from reality and irrelevant subplots." Here it is obvious that Fassbinder's intentions had not been understood: the film was not intended to be a documentary on factual conditions, but sought to demonstrate protypical possibilities for people to be able to triumph over existing circumstances through knowledge, courage and solidarity. Only a few critics understood this intention: "All the necessary and useful documentary efforts of Erika Runge, Gunthar Walraff, and (Rolf) Schubel/(Theo) Gallehr to bring the world of the worker into focus have not brought about as great a change of consciousness as the concentrated learning processes packed into the seemingly broadly and naively painted family idyll of Fassbinder's series." (Klaus Rainer Rohl, *konkret,* No. 26, Nov. 9, 1972, p. 45)

Fassbinder had deliberately made use of the cliches of the culture industry in his series, which was in contradiction to the basic ideas of the neo-Marxist media theory of Theodor W. Adorno, whose work had influenced the new German film critics (and the selfawareness of the younger German filmmakers) more than that of any other theoretician. Therefore, it is understandable why the series was attacked so vigorously by liberal and left critics alike.

Surprisingly, *Eight Hours Are Not a Day* was discontinued, despite earlier announcements. Dr. Gunther Rohrbach, head of television feature programming for the Westdeutscher Rundfunk, justified the cancellation of the series on "dramaturgical grounds": the projected episodes included so many long discussions about trade unions that the entertainment value would have suffered. "We should not be satisfied with this explanation, because the basis (for the cancellation) is at heart exactly what the critics of the series found lacking—the entering of the hitherto-absent trade unions into the depicted labor struggles.'' (Gunther Pflaum, *Funk-Korrespondenz*, No. 22, May 30, 1973, p. 13)

Fassbinder: ''I won't say anything about it. What are 'dramaturgical grounds'? You can blame it on dramaturgical grounds if you like. There are such things: Monika would have committed suicide, and the relationship between Marion and Jochen would have run into the kind of problems that Rohrbach didn't want—Rohrbach had an idea of them as 'that dream couple.' But this would have been a marriage with great difficulties. We would also have attempted to discover a utopian possibility, and how it *could* work, all right. Then, there would have been very concrete things: what the story has to say about these workers' organizations, what's happening to work councils and trade unions, here, we would have been somewhat more blatant than the Communist Party and somewhat more human than any system. For example, we wanted to say that the trade union is something that really doesn't have anything to do with the people any more, and that if the unions were to be able to do anything for people, they would have to return to fundamentals. That's an example of something that, from all accounts, you are not allowed to say so simply and straightforwardly. So it was all these things together, the dramatic complications, this analysis of things, on the one hand, and on the other, this political, but broader, perspective—but always very human, always seen very much from a human point of view—that undoubtedly made them decide to cancel it...'' (Interview, Feb. 20, 1974)

In Fassbinder's series the conventional separation in art between private life and the workplace is overcome: here, the problems of the work world are carried over into the private, and not the reverse, which is generally the case in art when work problems are depicted. In political documentaries, the onesideness is often reversed, and only the workplace is shown, while private life is seen, falsely, as a largely unproblematic appendage of life at work. Only a few works in the history of political cinema have successfully made a consistent connection between the two domains.

Fassbinder's series, in which—contrary to most political documentaries—people appear not as victims, but as possible masters of their own history is, as far as I can see, the only recent German film which understands enlightenment not as the statement of an enlightened author to like-minded people, but as educational work which directs itself to the consciousness of the unenlightened.

World on Wires (1973)

Part 1. At the Institute for Cybernetics and Future Research, political, social and economic events of the future can be simulated exactly by computer, as if they were happening today. The director of the research project, Vollmer (Adrian Hoven) commits suicide under mysterious circumstances. His successor is his erstwhile closest colleague, Dr. Fred Stiller (Klaus Lowitsch), who doesn't believe Vollmer killed himself. He maintains that the security agent of the Institute has disappeared without a trace. Stiller must struggle against pressure from the Hartmann Steel Company, which wants information about the production of steel for the next twenty years. Eva Vollmer (Mascha Rabben), the professor's daughter, assists Stiller in his investigations into her father's death.

Part 2. Gradually, Stiller begins to understand. Even the seemingly real world in which he lives is only another simulation made by a computer. This realization makes Stiller dangerous, and his arrest is ordered. He flees. He meets Eva, who loves him. She tells him, "I am only the projection of a real Eva from the real world." She establishes contact between the two worlds. At the same moment in which Stiller is shot by the police in front of the Institute, he finds himself with Eva, who has transferred his consciousness to another world.

This complicated story, the ramifications of which are not fully rendered, is told in the film in an amazingly simple way, as a compact and very action-oriented adventure film. The world we see is hardly any different from ours: it is made of steel and glass, just as our own office buildings and institutes are today. As in Godard's *Alphaville*, of which the decor is reminiscent, this is not a future world, but our own, once removed, so that we are made to believe that it isn't real, but only a simulation, a projection, of the real world. It is only a paradigm, but similar (not just externally) to our reality, because it can not spring beyond the limits of human thought. In this sense, the film depicts, actually quite anachronistically, the lonely battle of an individual against corruption and terror, and salvation through love. Outer appearances are secondary. As Mascha Rabben commented, "Basically, Klaus Lowitsch plays Humphrey Bogart, and I play Lauren Bacall."[1] Like the aforementioned film (Howard Hawks' *The Big Sleep*), Fassbinder's *World on Wires* makes a division between the density of the atmosphere and the intricacy of the story.

The novel, by Daniel F. Galouye, is more pessimistic; in it, the characters are more at the mercy of the system, of fate. Fassbinder has opposed this fatalism with the power of resistance.

1. Brochure, *Fernsehspiele Westdeutscher Rundfunk*, July-Dec., 1973, p. 69.

Fear Eats the Soul (1973)

When she seeks haven from a rainstorm in a bar frequented by foreigners, sixtyish Emmi Kurowski (Brigitte Mira) meets a Moroccan worker, Ali (El Hedi Ben Salem), who is at least twenty years her junior. Ali dances with Emmi, they talk together, and she invites him home for supper. Ali is attracted to Emmi, and eventually they get married. Their associates find their marriage incomprehensible. Emmi's three married children are ashamed, the neighbors gossip, and the grocer (Walter Sedlmayr) banishes Emmi from his establishment. Even Emmi's friends at work snub her. When the couple return from a vacation, they are surprised by the sudden friendliness displayed by the children, the neighbors and colleagues. However, the change comes out of social considerations. Now they all take advantage of Emmi. As the

Fear Eats the Soul

outer pressure on Emmi and Ali lessens, interior tensions become more evident. Ali returns to visit his old girlfriend Barbara (Barbara Valentin), the proprietor of the bar where he met Emmi, although admittedly with a bad conscience. When Emmi comes to the bar to bring Ali home, they dance (as at the beginning of the film), and he collapses. At the hospital, a gastric ulcer is discovered, which, as the doctor says, is common among immigrant workers because of the stress under which they live. Even if his health improves, Ali could suffer a relapse within six months. Emmi decides to try to prevent that from happening.

Fassbinder had carried this story around in his head for a long time. In *American Soldier* it is told by Margarethe, the chambermaid who later kills herself, but with a different ending. "And one day Emmi was found dead. Murdered. And on her neck was the imprint of a signet ring. The police arrested her husband, whose name was Ali and who wore a signet ring with an 'A' on it. But he said that he had a lot of friends named Ali, and that they all had signet rings. Then they questioned all the Turks in Hamburg named Ali,[1] but

Fear Eats the Soul

many were back in Turkey and the others didn't understand anything.'' What in *American Soldier* was consistent with the pessimism of the earlier films and still could be seen as a more personal love tragedy, is now, in *Fear Eats the Soul,* enriched by everyday experience. Fassbinder had already dealt frequently with marginal groups in society, especially in the gangster films, but never before had he described the characters so accurately and sympathetically, without sentimentality, in their need and helplessness, with their hopes and desires for a little bit of happiness. Even though the children, neighbors and co-workers serve within the rigorous dramatic requirements of the film, only more or less as captiongivers, the protagonists Emmi and Ali are shown with all their contradictions. Emmi and Ali, who themselves don't quite understand why they fell in love and got married, must muster the courage to change in small but determined ways. When Emmi wakes up after her first night in bed with Ali, she is frightened. Here it becomes strikingly clear ''how deeply prejudices are rooted, even in those who suffer from them.'' (Peter Buchka, *Suddeutsche Zeitung,* Mar. 4, 1974)

Fear Eats the Soul is also a variation on Douglas Sirk's *All That Heaven Allows* (1955). Of course, Fassbinder wasn't aware of this melodrama when he told the story in *American Soldier,* but he was familiar with it by the time he made this film. In *Heaven,* a rich widow (Jane Wyman) falls in love with a gardener (Rock Hudson) who is much younger than she and far below her socially. As in Fassbinder's film, she is held in contempt by those around her, including her own children. And as in *Fear Eats the Soul,* there is a bit of hope at the end, but no traditional "happy ending." In both films, there is an "impossible" love story, the ideal requirement for melodrama. But while Sirk depicts more generally the narrowness of a small American town (showing the numbness of life in the Eisenhower years as accurately as was possible in a Hollywood film), Fassbinder indicates the social origins of the prejudice encountered by his couple. Above all in the second half of the film, which departs from Sirk's story, where the prejudice turns to calculating condescension, Fassbinder demonstrates a sharper perception.

1. The working title of the film was *All Turks Are Named Ali.*

Martha (1973)

Thirtyish Martha Hyer (Margit Carstensen) is on vacation in Rome with her father (Adrian Hoven). The father suddenly collapses and dies on the Spanish Steps. At the German Embassy, Martha meets Helmut Salomon (Karlheinz Bohm), about forty-five years old. Some time later, she meets him again at the wedding of a mutual friend. As when they first met, Helmut exerts an immediate and powerful fascination over her. They soon marry. While still on the honeymoon, Helmut begins his "educational expedients" on Martha. After the trip, he rents a palatial house, in which he increasingly isolates her. She must renounce all contact with the outside world, in order to become entirely his creation. His affection is not without touches of sadism; his kisses resemble those of a vampire. In Helmut's absence, Martha begins meeting secretly with Kaiser (Peter Chatel), a young colleague from the library where she once worked. Helmut finally orders her not to leave the house. She feels threatened by him, and becomes convinced that he wants to kill her. She meets Kaiser again. While they are riding in his automobile, she is sure she is being followed. She begs Kaiser to speed up, and he loses control of the car. Martha survives the crash, but is crippled. Kaiser is killed. Helmut brings her home from the hospital in a wheelchair. Now she is totally his.

Martha is a "trivial" horror-version of *Effi Briest.* The parallels are extensive: the house Helmut rents is similar to the haunted house in Kessin; someone was once murdered there. Both rivals die—one in a real, the other in an imaginary duel. Martha (like Effi) remarks about her husband, "He has such stubborn principles." What Effi only suggests in a conversation with her mother ("... there was something strange about him. And he was also strange when he was being affectionate. Yes, then most of all. There were times when I was afraid.") is brutally obvious in *Martha:* Helmut repeatedly attacks his wife. The motivations of the two men are to be sure, partially different. While Innstetten feels compelled to behave as he does because of social norms, the Martha/Helmut drama is enacted on a more psychological level. Martha also enters into marriage inexperienced and virginal, but she is more fascinated by her husband, more directly in his power. During the first encounter in Rome, the camera completely encircles Martha and Helmut, pulling them into a vortex from which they can no longer escape. As much as Martha rebels against her husband's oppression, she seems secretly to long for subjugation. Fassbinder notes, "Martha is not really oppressed, but educated. And this education is like oppression... If Martha is no longer capable of living on her own at the end of the film, then she has achieved what she really wanted... The film tells a story that goes like this: What would make this woman happy? Most men can never oppress women as perfectly as they would like." *(Fernsehspiele Westdeutscher Rundfunk,* Jan.-July, 1974, p. 77ff.)

Of all Fassbinder's films, this seems to me to be the most compact, a film without digressions, resolutely aiming at a point. In the beginning, Martha lives in a situation of dependency upon her parents, who tolerate it. With her mar-

Martha

riage to the distinguished Helmut Salomon, a world seems to open up for her—but the hope proves fallacious. Her life becomes more and more confined, until in the end it is reduced to one point: the wheelchair. She is totally subjugated (or absolutely safe?). If the story were to continue, it might turn out that now she assumes domination.

With *Martha* Fassbinder moved a bit closer to realizing his ambition to make Hollywood films.

Effi Briest (1972-74)

Seventeen-year-old Effi Briest (Hanna Schygulla) marries Baron Geert von Innstetten (Wolfgang Schenck), a man twenty years her senior. Effi feels isolated in her new home, a small resort town on the North Sea. She is unhappy, without ever really admitting it to herself, because she realizes that she doesn't love her dogmatic, ambitious husband, despite a certain attachment. A break in the monotony, and then confusion, ensue when she makes the acquaintance of the new

Effi Briest

district commander, Major Crampas (Ulli Lommel), who also becomes friendly with her husband. A relationship develops between Effi and Crampas that oscillates between flirtation and passion. This ends when the Innstetten family moves to Berlin. Six years later, Innstetten accidentally discovers evidence of the earlier relationship between Crampas and his wife. He challenges Crampas to a duel and kills him. He divorces Effi, but retains custody of their daughter Annie, whom he alienates from her mother. Effi's will to live and vitality are broken, and she dies about a year later.

Fassbinder follows Fontane's novel closely. There are no alterations or additions; if anything, there is a concentration. *Effi Briest* is practically a two-character film. It is constructed around single sentences and scenes from the novel. Even before the wedding Effi says of her fiance, "He is so dear and good to me, and so patient, but...I'm afraid of him." Innstetten's attempts to educate her, especially as Effi sees them under the influence of Crampas, only reinforce this fear. Innstetten does not hesitate to frighten his wife with ghost stories about the house they inhabit in Kessin—to make use of the ghost as a means of education, or, better, as "a calculated fear-apparatus." On her deathbed Effi says that she misunderstood Innstetten, that he was right about everything. "Because he had so much good in his nature and was as noble as anyone can be who is without true love."

Fassbinder has probably never handled his protagonists as fairly as he does in *Effi Briest,* and in this he follows Fontane's example. Innstettin, whom we could see (even if contrary to the novel) as an absolute monster, is shown very differently by Fassbinder: after he discovers Effi's relationship with Crampas, he discusses the matter with Councillor Wullersdorf (Karlheinz Bohm). He is a man full of doubts; after six years, can it still be justified to challenge Crampas to a duel? He is a man full of despair in his later admission that "My life is ruined." Fassbinder's decision to concentrate wholly on this relationship between Innstetten and Effi has inevitable consequences: certain subplots and motifs of the novel had to be sacrificed. Effi's female friends in Hohen-Cremmon and the neighbors in Kessin now appear only on the margins. Even Geishubler and Crampas remain colorless. The various relationships in which the couple are involved, and which are a factor in their lives, as well as their parties and excursions, can be deduced from spoken allusions and plot details, but are seldom shown. Nevertheless, Fassbinder's decision, which makes the story more abstract, seems to me the correct one. This concentration allows for the depiction of at least one, the most important, story line in the novel, with all its necessary nuances (despite the film's excessive length of 143 minutes).

Still, it should be asked how this undertaking is justified. Is the film, even if extraordinarily tasteful, only a digest-version of a great novel? For me, Fassbinder's accomplishment lies primarily in the fact that he has reconstructed a historical period with more care than has been the case in any other German film (with the exception of Straub's *Chronicle of Anna Magdalena Bach*) in recent years, retaining all the strangeness that this period should have for us today. The eighty years which lie between Fontane's novel (1895) and our own day are consciously emphasized. Fassbinder augmented this feeling by shooting the film in black and white,

Effi Briest

with a slightly less sensitive film stock, as would have been used in the days of silent films. It is characterized by a great depth of focus and an extraordinary abundance of subtle nuances between black and white, which required, to be sure, artificial sources of light, not only for the interior shots, but also to a degree for the exteriors. The light in *Effi Briest* is even and tranquil, and gives the space plasticity and forcefulness. Fassbinder does not fade out at the end of a sequence (to black) but "in" (to white), contrary to traditional methods. Each new sequence begins with white leader, then the opening of the lens is gradually reduced until the right exposure is reached. Therefore, each detail of the often short sequences suddenly appears like a fragment out of memory.

The film has a tranquil rhythm. In many scenes, especially at the beginning and the end, the actors play their parts without speaking, while an unseen narrator (Fassbinder) recites Fontane's text. This rather unusual procedure is also conducive to placing a distance between the spectator/listener and the narrative.

Fassbinder never worked as long on a film as he did on this

one (58 shooting days), with a year-long interruption when the leading actor Wolfgang Schenck became ill. This painstaking care produced the coolest, most artificial of his films so far, if we disregard the stylization of the gangster films —especially the artificial language. However, *Effi Briest* is never sterile. The film derives its intensity from the tension between aloofness (in the form of the narrative) and emotion (in the content of the story).

Fox and His Friends (1975)

Munich, 1974: Franz Biberkopf (Fassbinder), an unemployed carnival performer whose act was called "Fox, the Talking Head," is introduced to a group of fashionable homosexuals by Max (Karlheinz Bohm), an art and antique dealer. Here he meets Eugen (Peter Chatel), the son of a businessman. They fall in love, and Eugen breaks with his lover Philipp (Harry Baer). Eventually, they take an apartment together, which the cultivated Eugen decorates, but which is paid for by Franz, who has just won about half a million Marks in a lottery. Moreover, Franz saves the printing factory owned by Eugen's parents (Adrian Hoven, Ulla Jacobsen) from bankruptcy with a loan of 100,000 DM. Eugen gets Franz to dress fashionably and attempts to teach him refined manners, proper grammar and an appreciation for culture. However, the class and educational differences between the two prove unsurmountable. Franz is finally wiped out by Eugen; he loses his share of the factory and his title to the apartment. Franz and Eugen separate. Eugen doesn't take it too hard—Philipp comes back to him—but Franz dies of an overdose of pills.

In the entrance hall of the Marionplatz Station of the Munich subway, which is totally empty except for Franz's lifeless form, two small boys appear. They take what is left of the dead man's money out of his pockets. The art dealer and one of Franz's earlier lovers pass by, but they hurry away so as not to become involved in the death.

Although the entire male contingent of Fassbinder's "ensemble" appear in featured and smaller roles, *Fox* is, like

Fox and His Friends

Martha and *Effi Briest,* again a two-character film. Two men meet by chance; they are fascinated with one another precisely because of their different backgrounds; this enchantment doesn't last long—class and cultural distinctions break through it. Eugen turns into the teacher, Franz submits. The *Martha* prototype is played out again, with variations.

In its first half, *Fox* brings a new tone into Fassbinder's work: in spite of occasional clownish-comic elements in earlier films, Fassbinder had never carried a comic style as far as he does here. Laconic dialogue aimed at punch lines, comically sharpened situations (the race to the lottery to make it before closing time), irony: none of Fassbinder's other films have as much freedom and detachment as the first part of *Fox and His Friends.* Even the relaxed playing out of the homosexuality, which had always been a latent element, especially in the early Munich gangster melodramas, seems here to take on a cheerfulness and taken-for-granted quality that is new. Yet, in the second half, Fassbinder returns to his familiar melodramatic methods. The more the relationship between Franz and Eugen becomes strained, the

Fox and His Friends

more strongly Franz comes to the fore as the favored identification-figure. His fear, his rage, his unhappiness, determine the rhythm of the film more and more, and its spontaneous lightness is diminished accordingly. The comically exaggerated characters of the first half develop, because of this, a posterlike overdistinctness, which takes a great deal away from their authenticity. Eugen turns into an arrogant fop and malicious villain, Franz into a bumbling fool who never catches on to what's happening to him—both comic strip figures. Along with the comic elements, the depicted situations also lose their precision. The many and varied humiliations of Franz by Eugen always follow the same pattern, which eventually becomes tiresome. The tragic ending, Franz's suicide and the looting of the corpse by the children (which nothing in the film prepares us for), possesses the same heaviness we recognize from the earliest films; when contrasted with the first half of the film, the impact here becomes even more intense and penetrating.

Fox stimulates speculations as to interpretation. For the first time in five years, Fassbinder again plays a leading role, the most extensive so far in his films. It seems to me that Fassbinder wants to depict here, in a distanced way, his experiences with German cultural life: his rise out of the counter-culture; the condescension mixed with enthusiasm with which the proletarian *enfant terrible* was greeted by the Cogniscenti; the exploitation of his talent by the culture industry, and the loss of freedom and spontaneity resulting from accomodation to its traditional norms. In contrast to the film, however, the end in real life remains open.

Mother Kusters' Goes to Heaven (1975)

The film begins like a continuation of *Why Does Herr R Run Amok?* Hermann Kusters, for twenty years a worker in the same factory in Frankfurt, shoots a supervisor and then himself, in protest over threatened mass firings. His wife, Mother Kusters (Brigitte Mira) is at first helpless in face of the disaster. Her son Ernst (Armin Meier) and even more his wife Helene (Irm Hermann) turn away from her, not wishing to become involved publicly in the "factory murder scandal"; her daughter Corinna (Ingrid Caven), a nightclub singer, uses the unforeseen publicity to further her career. A magazine reporter (Gottfried John) who seemed more sympathetic than the others who were hounding the family, writes an especially sensationalistic, slanderous article. On the other hand, she gets consolation from Karl Thalmann (Karlheinz Bohm), a journalist for the Communist Party newspaper, and his wife Marianne (Margit Carstensen). The couple tell her that her husband's act was wrong in its method, but understandable given his reason; the act was the result of decades of oppression on the job and a protest against the threatened firings. She joins the Communist Party. At a meeting, she explains her motive: she feels that here, she is taken seriously. She laments that her husband didn't have people like these Communists, with whom he could have talked. "He was a man who fought back, because he had been beaten all his life. The way that he did it was wrong...but I will make amends." Mother Kusters hopes that the Party will rehabilitate her husband in the public eye, but

Mother Kusters Goes to Heaven

when they fail to do anything of the kind, she turns for help to an anarchist (Matthias Fuchs), who has promised to make an issue of her case through "public action." He stages a sit-in with his friends at the editorial offices of the magazine that had published the slanderous article. Terrified, in a trance-like state, Mother Kusters must stand by as the terrorists take hostages and demand the freedom of all political prisoners in the Bundesrepublik. On the way to the escape car provided by the police, an exchange of fire occurs, and a terrorist and Mother Kusters are killed.[1]

Mother Kusters Goes to Heaven is a pessimistic answer to to Piel Jutzi's well-known 1929 social-criticism film, *Mutter Krausens Fahrt ins Gluck (Mother Krausen's Trip to Happiness),* in which a resigned working-class woman who sees gassing herself as the only solution to her misfortunes, is contrasted to an effective workers' movement, which offers hope for the future. In Fassbinder's film, the Communist Party has deteriorated into a bourgeois party: Thalmann lives in an elegant house which his rich wife inherited; he meets friends

Mother Kusters Goes to Heaven

for discussions over a glass of wine; the Party meeting takes place in an art gallery hung with Old Masters; for this public appearance Thalmann changes into a leather jacket. Despite their genuine affection for Mother Kusters and their talk about socialism and solidarity, Thalmann and his wife ultimately only use the widow for their own purposes. On the other hand, the "anarchists" who suddenly appear at the end of the film offer no alternative: their "action" is a mixture of dilettantism and idiocy. Mother Kusters is the only positive character in the film.She is not resigned; she gains consciousness and insight, even though she never breaks out of the limits of individual protest. She remains on the threshold of politics.

Fassbinder's perspective is very similar to that of his heroine. He also measures the quality of the depicted leftist (or "leftist") groupings by their public performance in the face of a spectacular "affair". As interesting as the evaluation of such a case might be, an analysis of left political groups when they become involved in the everyday work of organization, tenants' initiatives, child rearing, etc., might have been more illuminating and absorbing. *Mother Kusters* is, despite formalistic advances, still a step backward from the television series *Eight Hours Are Not a Day*. It is the politically-minded film of an apolitical director.

With *Martha,* this is Fassbinder's most cohesive narrative film. The meaning is identical with the film (for this reason, the detailed synopsis). How well Fassbinder has told his story is obvious at the beginning and the end of the film—Hermann Kusters' act and the bloodbath which ensues after the hostage taking—events which would have been not only difficult to film but which were extraneous to the theme—are not shown, but only told to us, the murder and suicide through a radio news report, and the shootout in a newspaper headline.

1. Fassbinder reshot his original "tragic" ending, replacing it with a more ironic one. In the present version, the "anarchists" not only do not take hostages, but become so demoralized when their "action" fails to attract the expected press coverage that they leave. Mother Kusters refuses to go with them, and continues her sit-in alone, until a janitor, a widower of her own age, expresses solidarity with her and invites her to his home to share a sausage and potato dish he calls "heaven and earth." Mother Kusters has possibly been Fassbinder's most politically controversial film: even some of his erstwhile supporters on the left took offense at his negative portrayals of the Communist Party and/or the radical youth movement. (R. M.)

Fear of Fear (1975)

Margot Staudte (Margit Carstensen), a young woman, married, with a daughter and a second child born at the beginning of the film, suffers from attacks of anxiety which are as incomprehensible to her as is her environment. She gets no help from her family. Her husband Kurt (Ulrich Faulhaber) is sympathetic in his way, but weak, thinking only about an examination he has to pass, and her mother- and sister-in-law (Brigitte Mira, Irm Hermann) only feel embarrassed by Margot's strange behavior. A pharmacist (Adrian Hoven) who gives her Valium without a prescription only sees her as

a possible candidate for an affair. Her doctors are perplexed—one diagnoses schizophrenia and another, a woman, deep depression. They recommend work as therapy. The only two people who have any contact with the more and more isolated Margot are on the edge of society: her little daughter Bibi (Constanze Haas) and a "crazy" neighbor, Mr. Bauer (Kurt Raab), whose repeated question, "Can you talk to anyone *else*?" she cannot bring herself to answer. Finally a hearse comes for Mr. Bauer, who has hanged himself. Margot seems unaffected, but at the end of the film, after the credits, the image dissolves once again, signalling a new attack of anxiety.

After the overambitious and consequently not very effective *Mother Kusters Goes to Heaven, Fear of Fear,* based on a story by the Schweinfurt housewife Asta Scheib and produced for the Westdeutscher Rundfunk, is impressive for its simplicity and unpretentiousness. It is a portrait of a depressive housewife seen from her point of view, a further development of *Martha* (and *Herr R*), and at the same time a cancellation of both. In these earlier films, the psychosomatic disorders, the inability to live, the fear, are still decidedly derived from life-situations. In *Fear of Fear,* Fassbinder abandons some crutches: Margot's fear is not clearly stated. Certainly, many of the elements which contribute to her fear are discernible, but the equation "because this is so, this must also be" is avoided. The narrative style corresponds with this: there are no main or side plots in the story; everything is equally important and unimportant. The narrative is not aimed toward a destination; there is no dramatic theory at work here. Individual observations are situated side by side, and sometimes one sequence can be interchanged with another. This simultaneity coincides perfectly with the subject of the narrative. Only in this way does it become evident that this fear has no clearly perceptible cause, and was not brought on by any specific event, but that it also cannot be overcome by any other event. It persists, and is disturbing to the audience for precisely that reason.

This restraint ordains the repetition of the optical lines of the film. Time and again, Margot is shown in the same or similar shots; if she is alone in a room, the camera is often in

Fear of Fear

an adjoining room, so that she is seen framed by the doorway, a symbol (in relation to the narrative) of isolation and
imprisonment. Margot and Mr. Bauer are repeatedly shown
from above through a window, which serves likewise to cut
them off. Fassbinder's favorite device, the mirror shot,
serves a special function here: when Margot looks at herself
in the mirror, the "objective" camera which sees her from
the outside and the "subjective" camera which shows what
she sees, become identical. Last but not least, the constant
alternation between these two perspectives gives the film its
disquieting intensity. The image blurs (subjective camera)
repeatedly before Margot's eyes, signifying her fear; then she
is again observed (objective camera), but the image still
blurs, not only in the mirror image. Because of this, when
Margot passes by her image, she sees herself dissected and
becomes frightened by herself, while the spectator, conversely, turns into Margot, sees through her eyes, and discovers
his or her own experience intensified through Margot's.

The very deliberate but never mechanically-employed narrative and visual methods used by Fassbinder here come from

I Only Want You to Love Me

a familiar Hollywood tradition (especially Hitchcock), but he has integrated them here, as he, until now, has done only in *Martha,* into his own view of the world and humanity.

I Only Want You to Love Me *(1976)*

This is the story of a young man, Peter (Vitus Zeplichal), who tries to buy the love that has always been denied him. He builds a house for his parents (Erni Mangold, Alexander Allerson) in his spare time, he regularly brings his mother flowers, and buys his wife (Elke Aberle)—whom he married to escape the rigidity of his family—expensive furniture for the house, also pampering her with gifts and attentiveness. Soon he can no longer make the payments on the furniture. Then, when he loses his job on a construction site, he kills an innkeeper who reminds him of his father in a moment of confusion. He is sentenced to ten years in jail, where a psychiatrist (Erika Runge) attempts to discover something about his life and the reason for his act.

171

I Only Want You to Love Me

I Only Want You to Love Me could have been the title of almost any one of Fassbinder's films. It is clearly and resolutely the proper title for this film. The end is already predictible after a few scenes. Peter, to whom affection is never shown, with whom no one ever carries on a conversation that goes beyond empty words, and who is for this reason incapable of talking about himself, even to his wife, this Peter, who grew up during the time of the "economic miracle," has observed that relations between people follow the rules of exchange and the market. He adapts himself to this. Exclusively a victim in the beginning, he soon turns into an innocent/guilty accomplice. He has so internalized the laws of exchange that he cannot imagine love relationships in any other way. With this attitude, he puts everyone around him, especially his wife, under pressure: she can no longer develop a free relationship with him. The tragic ending, the murder of the ersatz-father, is in itself of consequence. Peter had been afraid of his father all his life, and had never contradicted him. A verbal liberation from this superego was not possible.

I Only Want You to Love Me is a modest film, tolerable

despite its noisiness because it avoids hysterical gestures. In a way, it belongs to the cycle of early gangster films, though it lacks their poetry. A simple step-by-step narrative: television. Fassbinder knows how to make the distinction between his theatrical and television films.

Satan's Brew (1976)

"The main character in this wild spectacle is Walter Kranz, once celebrated as the Poet of the Revolution, played splendidly and egomaniacally by Kurt Raab. Though all goes on as before, the fiery Bard has become silent. Now there remain only debts, a capable, nagging wife (Helen Vita), a feebleminded brother (Volker Spengler), and a hateful middle-class existence. After he murders his rich mistress, the poetic vein flows again, but takes the form of a plagiarism of Stefan George's *Albatross* poems, which were themselves originally, not free from the influence of Baudelaire. Though Kranz is enraged that his own family is accusing him of spiritual robbery, he "becomes" George. And as luck would have it, the savings of a middle-aged admirer, Andree (Margit Carstensen) make it possible for him to establish a poetic "circle," for which he hires himself a group of street hustlers to act as his "youthful followers," some of whom naturally take off soon afterwards, because they have to make money. Kranz, in the meantime quite the superman, robs his parents and a prostitute with whom he had wanted to make a book of interviews when his own words became obstructed. Now the images come whirling toward the end: his wife Luise dies, he is beaten up by the patron of the prostitute, he loses the admiration of Andree, the murder case will soon be solved, and his crazy brother, on whom he planned to pin the murder, shoots this incarnation of noble art. Finished? The bullets spatter fake stage blood. The terrible ending dissolves into a trick ending without terror—we are back at the beginning. Is this life?" (Peter Buchka, *Suddeutsche Zeitung*, Nov. 26, 1976)

It becomes more and more clear that *Effi Briest* was a turning point in Fassbinder's career. "I would have to continue,

Satan's Brew

then everything would become wonderful..." (Fassbinder, *Spiegel*, No. 29, 1977). At the time, I also admired his humane depiction of his characters, and hoped that he would continue on this course. Instead, Fassbinder has, ever since, left his fans, his audience, and a large number of critics more bewildered with each subsequent film. *Effi Briest* was not a beginning, but an end. That did not have to happen. The film, in retrospect, achieved very much the aura of a "classic"; it was certainly not an easy film, its provocations were merely more concealed than in later works; its success with the public was by no means foreseeable. It was, in its way, also a radical film, a personal film; the despair over the fate of Effi is simply not expressed as loudly as the accusations in later films.

If we place *Effi Briest* at one end of a scale, then *Satan's Brew* belongs at the other (with *Katzelmacher*, perhaps, in the middle). Wilfried Wiegand has said of *Satan's Brew*, "What makes the film fascinating is the undertone of deeper despair, almost hatred of humanity, which breaks through here, demolishing all the boundaries of good taste and nar-

Satan's Brew

rative culture. We sense that Fassbinder has in no way dreamed up these atrocious details and grotesque exaggerations in order for us to take them lightly as gags, or even to shock us. We understand, rather, that her is a reckless narrative style that doesn't take anything into consideration or concern itself about a point of view; it is as if someone were crying or shrieking or going around in a rage of despair, without worrying about whether his words were well-chosen or even clearly understandable to the ear.'' It is, he concludes, ''private suffering, advertised in a mass medium.''

If this is true, and I think it is, then the alienation between Fassbinder and his audience is understandable—and inevitable. It seems that Fassbinder has, in *Fox and His Friends* and *Mother Kusters,* but especially in *Satan's Brew,* partially forfeited his directorial precision (even if Pflaum's book on Fassbinder, *Das bisschen Realitat, das ich brauche,* doesn't confirm it), and where he gets it back—in *Chinese Roulette*—it produces, as far as I'm concerned, idle motion. Fassbinder's most recent films evade the judgments of the film critics, to a degree: how can I think of something to say about this despair and about its resulting self-pity (in the second half of *Fox,* in *I Only Want You to Love Me,* and in *Bolweiser*)?

I have so many difficulties with these films because for me, this rage, which could be productive, usually deteriorates into hysteria. Even *Satan's Brew,* the strongest of these films, has more braggadocio than real power. This certainly has something to do with Kurt Raab, who in his worst moments displays Punch-and-Judy-like inclinations.

If we reflect upon what brought about this change in Fassbinder's narrative and technical methods, we must satisfy ourselves with approximations, because public biography (personal biography is not under debate here) and artistic creation should not be equated, since generally the biographical only has contingent value as evidence in art. Nevertheless, Fassbinder's experiences in Frankfurt during the year he managed the Theater am Turm (1974-75) were something of a shock for him. The vehement rejection of his Frankfurt piece, *The Earth Is Unlivable, Uninhabitable as the Moon* by the Project Commission of the Film Funding Institute, the charges of anti-semitism prompted by his theatre piece *Der Mull, die Stadt und der Tod (Garbage, the City and Death),* which was withdrawn from publication by Suhrkamp Verlag (while the film version of the play, *Shadows of Angels,* directed by Daniel Schmidt—after protests in Cannes—opened relatively unnoticed and unchallenged in a few cinemas), the vehement rejection of almost all his films since *Effi Briest* by the critics (only Schutte, Pflaum and Blumenberg always defended him, as far as I can tell)—all this could surely upset a sensitive filmmaker like Fassbinder. His reaction, readable in his films, widened the gap even more. This alienation could no longer be stopped, was no longer reversible. Be that as it may, *Satan's Brew,* as controversial as the discussions were about it, had several critics rally to its side, among them Buchka, whose synopsis I have already quoted. He saw in the film ''an almost tranquil turnabout, which with cynical humor turns less upon defined grievances than upon an indistinct atmosphere so that the wreckage of reality flies into one's eyes.'' With the television film *Bolwieser,* Fassbinder had his first critical success in a long time.

Satan's Brew

At the same time Fassbinder was going through his crisis in Germany, his reputation abroad was growing; this success culminated in a commercial retrospective of his films in New York in the spring and summer of 1977. This exposition of his work was not in chronological order, but placed early and later films side by side. The traditional critic's question —"How does the new film compare with the last one?"— was therefore secondary: the basic elements of Fassbinder's work were sifted out. The retrospective opened with *Mother Kusters Goes to Heaven,* the least successful of Fassbinder's films in Germany. The New York reception was almost enthusiastic; the critics celebrated the film as a comedy, since a new ending had been added that lightened it considerably. Mother Kusters no longer dies, but finds practical solidarity with a janitor, after the ideologues with all their rhetoric fail to do anything.

Increasing difficulties in Germany, among them the rejection of the *Debit and Credit* project by the Westdeutscher Rundfunk, and growing recognition abroad, caused, or at least prompted, Fassbinder to announce in the summer of

Satan's Brew

1977 that he would leave Germany and in future work abroad, possibly in Hollywood. Since then, he has had a number of new assignments, and at least for now, there is no more talk of emigration.

Chinese Roulette (1976)

In Munich, a married couple take leave of one another for the weekend. She (Margit Carstensen) is going to Milan, he (Alexander Allerson) to Oslo. Instead, they meet again the same day at their castle in the country, she with her lover (Ulli Lommel) and he with his mistress (Anna Karina). Unexpectedly, their crippled daughter Angela (Andrea Schober) arrives later that evening with her mute governess (Macha Meril). These six are looked after by a housekeeper (Brigitte Mira) and her literary son Gabriel (Volker Spengler). After a period of uncertainty and self-searching, the inhabitants participate in a game arranged by Angela, who is more intelligent than her hated parents. The game, Chinese Roulette, is a kind of truth-game. The eight people divide themselves into two groups of four, and one group secretly chooses a member of the other group, the members of which must guess who it is by asking questions like "If this person were a wild animal, what kind would he be?" or "If this person went to live on a deserted island, what would she take with her—a person, a book or a thing?" or "What would this person have done in the Third Reich?" The answers, which are very diverse, tell more about the answerer than about the person who is "it". Nevertheless, it gradually becomes clear that Angela is putting her mother on the firing line with the game. The mother reacts to this provocation with a gun, but she shoots the governess, who is slightly wounded, rather than her daughter. After a confrontation between Angela and Gabriel in which she accuses him of plagiarism, we hear another shot, but have no way of knowing who is involved. The camera shows the castle from the outside, while a procession goes by. The image freezes.

In hardly any other film has Fassbinder communicated as little about his characters as in this one. There is only one basic constant: the hatred between the crippled Angela and her parents. But even the reason for these feelings remains obscure. There are, of course, some fragmented details about the previous lives of the characters, but these allusions are immediately thrown into doubt or turn into their opposite. Gabriel listens behind a door and discovers a detail which is also interesting to the audience; Angela catches him unawares. "The eavesdropper behind the door often hears false information," she tells him and the audience. But perhaps Angela is also lying at this moment. Many references remain enigmatic: in Paris the week before someone or other was murdered. "Now there are only two of us," the housekeeper tells the husband. The questions and answers in the Chinese Roulette game infer certain events in the past, but they are so ambiguous that they allow for any interpretation.

The most significant scenes in the film, especially the Chinese Roulette sequences, take place in a room full of mirrors and plexiglass panes. The characters often seem cut in half or doubled by them. A constantly moving camera breaks up the spatial perspective, establishing always new, always unstable

Chinese Roulette

connections between the characters. A script that is constructed down to the last detail according to the laws of
mathematics, not of life, stage direction that exorcizes the
individuality of the characters and produces artificial mon-
sters, can be interpreted in a variety of different ways (that is
the trick of the film). H. G. Pflaum (*Suddeutsche Zeitung,*
Apr. 22, 1977) perceived here "a mastery of narrative and of
emotions" and "control over his own rage, his own pessimism." Wolfram Schutte *(Frankfurter Rundschau,* Nov. 25,
1976) saw "intentionally open glass doors through which the
spectator can—and must—allow his fantasies to wander."
Even if we accept the craftsmanship of the production—in
fact *Chinese Roulette* is reminiscent of the virtuosity in some
of the sequences in *Beware of a Holy Whore,* there remains
the question of expenditure and effect. To me, *Chinese
Roulette* is a document on love and lovelessness, an exercise
in technique which certainly displays Fassbinder's powers as
a *metteur-en-scene,* but really nothing more. In the much
more crude *Satan's Brew* there are at least feelings to be
detected, which are even infectious, be it only because we of-

Chinese Roulette

fer resistance as spectators, whereas here there is nothing but brilliant emptiness.

Another observation comes to mind. This appears to be Fassbinder's first film produced explicitly for a world market. It is only by chance and in superficial appearance that the film takes place in Germany. Where the earlier films were either open or coded commentaries on conditions in the Bundesrepublik, this one takes place in No-man's Land.

Bolwieser (1976-77)

The small Bavarian town of Werburg in the 1920s. The Stationmaster Xaver Bolwieser (Kurt Raab), in his mid-thirties, is married to Hanni (Elisabeth Trissenaar), the daughter of a brewery owner. He is sexually dependent on her, and subjugates himself in other respects also to her orders and real or imaginary desires. This apparent harmony is shattered when Hanni takes up first with her onetime schoolmate, the innkeeper Merkl (Bernhard Helfrich) and then with the hairdresser Schafftaler (Udo Kier); she also has business dealings with both. Bolwieser does not want to accept reality; he commits perjury in order to defend his wife against the malicious gossip of the neighbors. When Hanni breaks with Merkl and demands back the money she lent him, he denounces the stationmaster to the authorities. Bolwieser is sent to prison for four years: left with nothing after his release, he takes lodgings with a ferryman (Gerhard Zwerenz) and finally assumes his job when he dies.

Oskar Maria Graf wrote his novel *Bolwieser* in 1931. Fassbinder made two versions of his adaptation of the book: a three-hour television film which is almost fastidiously faithful to the novel and a more freely adapted two-hour theatrical film. The central theme of both versions is the same: the slow destruction and self-destruction of a petty bourgeois individual by his wife, by small-town hypocrisy and jealousy, and by his own subservient mentality.

The television version lays the story out for the viewer in detail; Bolwieser and Hanni are surrounded by a gallery of George Grosz-like German philistines of the Bavarian variety. The theatrical version, on the contrary, concentrates wholly on the two-character drama of husband and wife, in which even Hanni's two lovers are nothing more than incidental figures. Hanni is more active and resolute. She, and no longer her father, gives Merkl the loan to open his inn in Werburg. The fusion between business and sexuality has never been more clear. The end is tighter and tougher than in the epically broad television version. Bolwieser refuses the reconciliation between himself and nature. The closing music, the alto solo from the Fourth Movement of Mahler's Second Symphony ("Der Mensch liegt in grosster Not") resounds no longer with mythical water-images reminiscent of Dreyer's *Vampyr* or Wysbar's *Fahrmann Marie,* but with the feelings of Bolwieser, who is led to his cell, gradually disappearing into the depths of the frame.

As closely as Fassbinder has followed Graf's story, in any event in the television version, the casting of the title role and the directorial methods make Bolwieser another unmistakable Fassbinder film. Kurt Raab's Bolwieser doesn't have much more in common with the goodnatured, but strong,

Bolweiser

hero of the novel than a middle class mentality. He is weak
from the beginning, a loser, while Graf grants his hero at the
beginning the composure of a "conquering hero." The
physical attraction between Xaver and Hanni is obvious in
the novel, but in the film, only alleged. What in Graf is a
headlong fall from grace becomes in Fassbinder the gradual
deterioration of a condition which had existed from the
beginning.

In the first half of the film, Hanni and Xaver are drawn
differently. Hanni's alienation from her husband shows signs
of emancipation. In the second half, however, the film takes
Bolwieser's position more and more. He is the disappointed,
deceived party, and all the sympathy goes to him. "Dismem-
bered! Torn to pieces! She has torn out my guts and trampled
on them!"—the painful words (which are also in the novel,
in an interior monologue) are cried out in jail in an outburst
of the deepest despair and isolation. Bolwieser continues the
long series of betrayed lovers who were usually played by
Fassbinder himself in the early films and again in *Fox and
His Friends.*

Bolweiser

One of the strong points of *Bolwieser* is the depiction of the social reasons for and results of the deformities of the main character and the people around him, especially his subordinates at the Railroad Station: if the callow petty bourgeois Bolwieser represents the type of subject upon whom the imminent Nazi regime can depend, then the underlings at the Station, one of whom already wears an S.A. uniform, represent the type of sadist also needed by the Third Reich for "special" tasks.

Women in New York (1977)

A group of women in New York in the 1930s occupy themselves with parties and trips to fashion shows, hairdressers and "figure salons". Their lives revolve around beauty and health—the wealthy men who pay for it all are never seen, but are the main topic of conversation. All the women are fixated on their husbands or lovers, and live through them and for them. Therefore it is a catastrophe for Mary Haynes

184

Women in New York

(Christa Berndl) when she discovers, thanks to the spying of her friend Sylvia (Margit Carstensen) that her husband Steven has a mistress, Chrystal (Barbara Sukowa), who is more interested in Steven's bank account than she is in him. Mary and Steven separate, and Chrystal becomes the new Mrs. Haynes. But Chrystal soon has a new lover. At a party a year after the divorce, Mary experiences a belated triumph: she is able to expose Chrystal in front of all her friends.

Fassbinder directed this successful 1936 play by the late author-politician Claire Booth Luce in the fall of 1976 at the Hamburger Schauspielhaus, and subsequently adapted and directed it for television with cameraman Michael Ballhaus. The women move around in rooms decorated in Art-Deco and are themselves turned into decorative objects, status symbols, who are differentiated from one another more by outward appearance (younger, older, prettier, plainer) than by personality. They are totally dependent upon the value-system of their men, but never rebel. They participate in games of intrigue, calumny, speculation and gossip, always at the expense of their women friends, never the men. This dependency, which exists not only in fact but in their minds, makes the play depressing. Fassbinder goes out of his way to make the women unsympathetic: he augments their hysteria to the point where it is insufferable. Because of the socially determined oppression of women, there is inevitable subjugation.

The Women's Ensemble of the Hamburger Schauspielhaus mastered the many roles in the twelve scenes of the play brilliantly. If I remember correctly, each scene was filmed without a break. Fassbinder employs conventional camera arrangements and only seldom is there an ironic visual commentary; the most obvious is in the first scene, in which we see in the foreground an aquarium full of fish while the incessantly chattering women play cards.

Despair (1977)

Hermann (Dirk Bogarde), a Russian emigre, owns a small chocolate factory in Berlin in the early 1930s. He is married to Lydia (Andrea Ferreol), a buxom, rather silly woman who is having an affair with her cousin Ardalion (Volker Spengler), a painter who is usually drunk and has no money. Hermann has fantasies in which he observes and follows his double, especially when he goes to bed with Lydia. One day he meets Felix Weber (Klaus Lowitsch), an unemployed actor whom he thinks is his double. He tries to enlist Felix in a plan: the two should change their clothes and identities. It is important for Hermann to be seen at two different places at the same time. Felix agrees (for 1,000 Marks). But hardly have the clothes been changed when Hermann shoots his (presumed) double. He hides out in Switzerland, hoping to start a new life as Felix Weber. His plan fails; the two men looked nothing alike. After a short chase through hotels and pensions, Hermann is finally arrested.

No other film by Fassbinder is based on as polished and literate a script as Despair. Tom Stoppard's script (based on a novel by Nabokov) plays upon the *doppelganger* theme, with all the ambiguity of feeling and values of the final years of the Weimar Republic. Fassbinder follows the Stoppard

Despair

book fairly closely; he establishes a visual equivalent for
Stoppard's language, in which the *doppelganger* theme is extended even farther than in the script.

Despair is a film about fleeing, about escape. Hermann
and Lydia's home, modern for its time, full of glass walls and
mirrors (a paradise for voyeurs), is turned into a labyrinth by
the continually circling camera. The first encounter between
Hermann and Felix takes place in the mirror chamber of an
amusement park (in the script, Hermann suddenly sees, as he
looks into the water, his own face next to him). Even the office in the chocolate factory and the post office where Hermann receives mail addressed to "Pushkin" turn into mazes,
due to the combined effects of the decor and the camera.

In *Despair* there is no firm standpoint, no definable attitudes or actions; everything is in movement, interchangeable.
In Hermann, a man without qualities, without a homeland,
the era finds its perfect expression. The *doppelganger* theme,
fluctuating between psychology and politics, is dealt with on
varying levels; it permeates the film with changing refrac-
tions. Hermann is the double of Hermann. The double

Despair

fulfills his sexual desires, for which Hermann does not not accept responsibility. When Fassbinder abandons all his photographic tricks, the spectator loses perspective: which is Hermann and which is the double? Felix is Hermann's double, at least in Hermann's eyes. We know better from the beginning (and more precisely than by reading the script): outside of a vague resemblance, there is no similarity between Hermann and Felix.

Cinema is the double of reality: deception is part of its essence. Hermann sees a film (his double is sitting behind him) about twins, one a policeman, the other a gangster. Both die. Hermann, Lydia and Ardalion discuss how the film deceives the audience by splicing together two independently shot strips of film: they look for the line of partition on the screen.

The Nazis are the doubles of the democrats (or their vampires). When the Social Democrat Muller is defeated as Chancellor in March 1930, the National Socialist Muller (Peter Kern), an employee of Hermann's, comes to the office for the first time in his brown shirt. He had already earlier

Despair

grown a little Hitler moustache. S. A. members smash show windows; later they sit quietly in a sidewalk cafe. In the same cafe two Jews play chess at a table. Near the end of the film two Germans with shaven necks play there.

Despair is not an exact replica of history; it couldn't be if it wanted to. But Fassbinder has grasped the fluctuation and instability of the pre-Nazi era in striking images and constellations. He has proven himself as a director with unfamiliar material. The new actors, especially the brilliant Dirk Bogarde, bring irony and ambivalence to the film. At the end, Fassbinder's obsessions come breaking through again: after Hermann has shot Felix (which he was hesitant about to the end—which is not true in the book), after he has freed himself in this way from his double, his increasingly tiresome existence, then his sufferings begin, and persist until his capture. Suddenly the film comes to rest; patiently Fassbinder follows the trail of his hero, as the noose gradually tightens. The other characters, the other threads in the story, fade into the background. In his working-class clothes, which he took from Felix, Hermann gradually becomes the lonely gangster hunted by the police: Dirk Bogarde becomes the double of Humphrey Bogart.

Germany in Autumn (1978)

In this film, which was produced by several German directors, Fassbinder's episode, which follows immediately after the introductory documentary footage on Schleyer's funeral, offers a strong personal statement. It determines the climate of the film, the despair of the individual, but is also based upon the political situation.

In a cavelike apartment, which is never brightened by a ray of light, Fassbinder, who plays himself, lives with his friend, Armin Meier, whom he treats like a piece of shit. Fassbinder smokes dope, is frightened, is constantly on the phone. This is intercut with passages from a conversation with his mother, who allows her son to provoke her into declarations of "good common sense": for every hostage, a terrorist should be killed; an authoritarian ruler would be better than a democracy, but he should, of course, be "good". Fassbinder argues against the intervention of the State.

This very quickly made 30-minute film (done at the end of October, 1977, under the impact of the Schleyer assassination, Mogadishu, and the suicides at Stammheim) illustrates more than any of the other segments of Germany in Autumn the feeling of powerlessness experienced by a leftwing intellectual. It is not the political discussions that give this half hour its importance, but the brutality and honesty with which Fassbinder deals with himself as a man and a director: "For example, what I think is good in Germany in Autumn is the sequence by Fassbinder. There I would say, there is someone who just doesn't need an object or a symbol for his own problems, but he exposes himself to a situation. Not only as a man, but also as an artist. He admits his fear and shows us his messed-up relationship. That this happens with a man, I find the most political thing in the whole film. For someone to make such a film at such a time is daring. So I would say that Fassbinder has learned something from women. This is the way we can come to grips with things in a wholly unideological way.'' *(Helke Sander, quoted by Christa Maerker, Conversation with Helke Sander and Margarethe von Trotta, Jahrbuch Film 1978/79,* Munich: 1978)

The Marriage of Maria Braun (1978)

In a registry office that has just been hit by a bomb Hermann (Klaus Lowitsch) and Maria (Hanna Schygulla) Braun are married during World War II. After the end of the war, Maria, who works in a bar that caters to Americans, waits for her husband's return. A friend brings the news that he is dead. Maria becomes close to Bill, a black man who is kind and loving. When Hermann unexpectedly returns home from a prison camp, Maria kills Bill with a bottle. Hermann confesses to the crime and is sent to jail. Maria meets the manufacturer Oswald (Ivan Desny) and soon becomes indispensible to his textile firm, not only because of her knowledge of English, but because of her keen sense of business, which offers a new beginning in these still chaotic times. Oswald falls in love with Maria, who returns his affection, but refuses any kind of dependency. She only lives for the day when Hermann will be released from prison. When the moment comes, he disappears without a trace, and reappears suddenly after Oswald's death. At the reading of the will, Maria discovers that Hermann had made an agreement with Oswald to leave Maria alone as long as Oswald, who was already ill, was alive. Oswald has willed his fortune to the couple, half to Maria and half to Hermann. On July 4, 1954, while the reporter Herbert Zimmermann describes the final moments of a football game between West Germany and Hungary in Bern,the house explodes. Maria had not properly turned off a gas jet—deliberately or by accident?

This strongly melodramatic story (written by Peter Marthesheimer and Pea Frohlich from an idea by the director) is told more pointedly and simply than any film since *Martha.* Fassbinder abandons his previous stylization and overrefinements. Nevertheless, *The Marriage of Maria Braun* is a film rich in perspectives. Maria Braun, who is consistent in business and in love, who follows masculine rules, is not only

The Marriage of Maria Braun

portrayed as an individual, but as a symbol of her times. In revolutionary times, women are often more imaginative and enterprising. Maria sees herself as a "specialist in the future." In her relationships with men she always takes the initiative. "You don't have something with me," she tells Oswald, "the truth is that I have something with you." This is also a phenomenon which is seen in war and postwar periods, when women make decisions that men take away from them in "normal" times. It is a testimony to Fassbinder's great sense of the dramatic that he ends the story of Maria Braun on the day when Germany became the world champion in soccer: he added this to the script. This was the day the postwar period ended, and the Germans again felt themselves to be victorious. The end of the postwar period also brought about the end of the power of women. After the explosion, which was immediately preceded by Herbert Zimmermann's voice crying, "Germany is World Champion!," Fassbinder follows with the photographs of four politicians: Adenauer, Erhard and Kiesinger (in negative) and Schmidt (whose portrait develops from negative to positive: the

The Marriage of Maria Braun

postwar Chancellors of Germany, without Brandt. The men again hold triumph in their hands.

The film contains two major changes from the script: Fassbinder has indicated the historical background in other ways than the football game. Twice we hear Adenauer on the radio, the first time, he assures that there will be no rearmament; the second time he says that there must be rearmament. That politicians do not keep their word, that Germany is not a country to be trusted, are facts that Fassbinder establishes as having already been the case in the 50s. Fassbinder also changed the ending. While in the script, Maria kills herself and her husband by driving into a canyon, because she was deceived by him, whom she loved more than anything, the film leaves the question open. Accident or suicide? It is not clearly decided.

The Marriage of Maria Braun is the third film by Fassbinder in a short period of time that deals with German history. The Third Reich is circumvented: *Bolwieser* and *Despair* take place in different milieux at the end of the Weimar Republic; *Maria Braun,* after the war. This accumulation of films,

The Marriage of Maria Braun

which certainly did not come about by accident after Fassbinder's announcement that he was leaving Germany—
and his next big project, *Berlin Alexanderplatz,* also fits into
this pattern—directs our attention back to earlier works
which also dealt with Germany, for example, *Merchant of
the Four Seasons,* the first big film about the Adenauer
years, or *Mother Kusters Goes to Heaven,* the ill-tempered,
unfair settling of accounts with German left groups of all
shades.

Fassbinder is interested in history in its broadest perspective. He sees more continuities—middle class consciousness,
the authoritarian mentality—than breaks with the past. The
singular position of *Maria Braun* in Fassbinder's work
therefore, lies perhaps in the fact that for the first time he
shows an advance beyond petty bourgeois mentality, that he
tells the story of an emancipation, even if it fails in the end.
And it is very significant for the film that Maria is destroyed
by a men's conspiracy, that in the series of portraits of Chancellors, who brought about the political failure of the woman
Maria, Willy Brandt, the immigrant, is missing.

The Marriage of Maria Braun

Even when Fassbinder wrestles with history, it is always dealt with in his films from a modern point of view. His critique of the German middle class, its weaknesses, its servility, its inability to love, its egotistical preoccupation with prosperity, runs through almost all his films as a leitmotif. The petty bourgeoisie of 1930, 1955 and 1975 are interchangeable. Germany is a country in which nothing has changed, in which the opportunities of 1945 are played out.

In a Year of 13 Moons (1978)

Frankfurt am Main, Summer, 1978: Elvira Weishaupt (Volker Spengler), who several years previously became a woman through a sex-change operation, looks back over her life: the childhood of the boy Erwin in a convent, the job as a butcher, the marriage to Irene (Elisabeth Trissenaar), the daughter of the owner of a slaughterhouse, and the operation in Casablanca—events in a life which has been a fruitless search for love. His present life is no less miserable: usually

In a Year of 13 Moons

accompanied by "Red Zora" (Ingrid Caven), a friendly prostitute, deserted by his lover Christoph Hacker (Karl Scheydt) Erwin wanders through a nightmarish Frankfurt, through penny arcades and skyscrapers owned by the entrepreneur Anton Saitz (Gottfried John), for whose sake Elvira originally had the operation. When even the other people who are close to him—his wife, his daughter (Eva Mattes), a journalist (Gerhard Zwerenz), fail to recognize Elvira's despair, she dies "of a broken heart" (Fassbinder).

Of all Fassbinder's personal films (like *Fox and His Friends* or *Satan's Brew*), this is by far the most radical. It is disconcerting precisely because of the concentration of his methods. There is no room for self-pity in this film, and any hysteria is cancelled by a despair that has perhaps never before been expressed as harshly in a German film. Volker Spengler as Elvira delivers himself up to the character in a manner which is only possible through total identification. He drives the character to such extremes that she becomes almost artificial, transcending the apparent naturalism of the interpretation.

In a Year of 13 Moons

Fassbinder worked on the film from July 28 until August 28, 1978, a few months after the suicide of his friend Armin Meier, who appeared with him in *Germany in Autumn*. Fassbinder not only wrote the script and directed, but was responsible for the sets and editing, and did the camerawork himself for the first time. Never before had he taken a film so fully into his own hands; hardly any other film is so much tied up with his life. The last five days in the life of Elvira Weishaupt become an elegy, sustained musically by Mahler (in the first sequence, which takes place in the "gay strip" in Frankfurt), organ music, Christmas songs, rock music (from the group "Suicide"). But the film is held together above all by a new (for Fassbinder) and bold free association between images, sound and editing. culminating in the slaughterhouse sequence in which Elvira shows "Red Zora" around his former workplace, and remembers something his lover Christoph Hacker, who was once an actor, taught him—the despairing, self-tormenting, final monologue of *Tasso*.

In a year with thirteen new moons, according to Fassbinder, overly emotional people are especially in danger. "It

In a Year of 13 Moons

often ends in personal catastrophe.'' 1978 was such a year. The fate of Elvira can not, therefore, be rationally analyzed or discussed in sociological terms; there is no ''guilty party'' in the traditional sense of the word. Nevertheless, our society is not absolved by Fassbinder from accountability for the individual. That the world—here symbolized by Frankfurt—has become a nightmare, a hell, is shown by Fassbinder in almost apocalyptic images. The uniformity of modern architecture bespeaks the anonymity of a search for happiness which only finds surrogates—in penny arcades and bars. Personal relationships are either reduced to business or dessicated. The story of Elvira, as exceptional and monstrous as it seems, is at heart therefore thoroughly mundane, and is pertinent even to ''normal'' lives. Love relationships are destroyed in our society; many people simply don't notice it and go on living.

If none of the people Elvira comes across in the last five days of her life can help her, it is not because they are not good people, but because they are too occupied with themselves, are themselves destroyed. They pass Elvira by, talking

In a Year of 13 Moons

to her or listening to her, but drawing away at decisive moments. Only when it is already too late do they all arrive, as if drawn by an invisible magnet, to Elvira's deathbed while the interview she had with a journalist plays on the tape recorder.

Elvira's real opponent is Anton Saitz: an extreme example of a man who was destroyed (in a ''concentration camp''), and who now destroys others by dealing in land speculation and brothels. He has become infantile, playing out scenes from Jerry Lewis films with his bodyguards. When Erwin became Elvira for his sake, Anton Saitz had laughed at him. When he meets him again, he only asks him to make coffee for him. Anton Saitz seems to have come out of Fassbinder's play, *Der Mull, die Stadt und der Tod*. There, too, an especially bloodsucking entrepreneur turns out to be a Jew, which resulted in charges of anti-semitism against Fassbinder. The accusation, it seems to me, was shortsighted. The destruction of a man, and this is Fassbinder's theme, can be so total that he turns from a victim into an oppressor. Of course, he needs the ''right'' environment: Frankfurt—in the most total sense;

201

In a Year of 13 Moons

our economic system, which caters to every form of speculation and exploitation.

In essence *In a Year of 13 Moons* is a balance, an ending,
an attempt to come to terms with the problems of his personal life, and the (final?) repudiation of Frankfurt (Fassbinder moved to Berlin in the winter of 1978-79). With his
aesthetic innovations, the director has worked out for
himself new possibilities for a freer association between image and sound, for polyphonic visions and narrations. One
sequence, which is reminiscent of Godard's *Numero Deux,*
combines news footage of Pinochet with a French dramatic
film, a porn film and a television interview with Fassbinder.
Combining different optical and accoustical symbols with
one another—not always as ultra-distinctly as in this sequence—Fassbinder opens, in many scenes in this film, a
cosmos for the audience, who must conquer it for themselves.

The Third Generation (1978-79)

Winter 1978/79 in West Berlin. A group of young people who are united by secret signals (Code word: "The world as will and idea") and blind activism more than by political conviction, go underground after their colleague Paul (Raul Gimenez), a professional assassin fleeing from Africa, is shot by the police. On Carnival Tuesday the young terrorists kidnap the owner of an American computer firm, Peter Lenz (Eddie Constantine).

The terrorists of the "third generation" have no more political motivation, according to Fassbinder. They act for the sake of action, but with their violence, they are the expression of the society out of which they come. The first generation was motivated by idealism and excessive sensitivity vis a vis the system; the second had at least understood the motives of the first, and often became its defenders. From this point of departure, how can anyone make a comedy, which is what *The Third Generation* is, by Fassbinder's own admission.[1]

The film displays a great disrespect, which actually only with difficulty conceals a tone of mourning. The detatchment with which Fassbinder, picking up a theme from his early gangster films, makes no distinction between the terrorists and the police, is questionable, but at the same time, has something liberating about it. Here there are no ideological curtains separating one side from the other. In this avoidance of a discussion of principles, whether of the psychological or political variety, lies the provocation of the film. The actions of one side or the other are never justified on the grounds of superior motives.

The comic machinery functions especially well when individual members of the group change their clothes and rehearse their new identities (''My name is Oskar Matzerath, born in...''). This almost frivolous view of a serious matter cannot, however divert our glance from Fassbinder's characteristic sorrow about betrayal, futility and death. The most naive member of the group, Bernhard von Stein (Vitus Zeplichal), observes with growing perplexity how a spy and agent provocateur, August Brem (Volker Spengler), delivers the others to their fates. In death, the characters win back their dignity, which they had lost by their terrorist games. When Franz Walsch (Gunther Kaufmann) who surely isn't given Fassbinder's old pseudonym by accident, visits the grave of his sweetheart, though he has been warned not to, and is shot down by the police, his death is reminiscent of the first scene in Bresson's *The Devil, Probably,* in which a young man arranges own his suicide in a cemetery. But while most of Fassbinder's films end in despair, this one permits a satiric ending after the melodrama, which the comedy serves to put into perspective.

The terrorists, now dressed in carnival costumes, rehearse a videotaped message with their hostage Peter Lenz (!) in their hideout. To throw the authorities off, they play a tape recording of subway sounds in the background. Peter Lenz grins almost insolently into the camera while he announces that he is a ''prisoner of the people.'' Things come full circle dramatically when we recall that in the first scene, he had complained to his associates in the U. S. that he is hardly selling any more computers in Germany since the cessation of

The Third Generation

terrorist activity. But that will change. Susanne Gast (Hanna Schygulla), a member of the group, is Lenz's secretary until she goes underground with the others.

People who have lost their political motivations can easily be used by others, according to Fassbinder. "That was the idea I had when I made the film. For example, it is not important whether there really ever was an entrepreneur who backed terrorist activities in order to sell more computers." [2] Fassbinder makes evident through his use of sound how little independent, how uninspired, how unfocused, this "third generation" really is. The radio is on almost all the time in the homes of the group members; we hear news about the metal workers' strike, about the upheaval in Iran, about the war between Vietnam and China (by this means, a specific time period is given to the film). But no one seems to pay any attention to this news. The second sound level, which includes television, music, and quotations from books, is occasionally noticeable. The dialogue—which conveys the sense of the story to the audience—is sometimes hard to understand in the sound mix, but in any case the conversations never go beyond banalities, and political subjects are never discussed.

Thus, Fassbinder continues what he began with *The Marriage of Maria Braun* and *In a Year of 13 Moons*: the use of sound becomes increasingly important. Its interplay with the images makes certain demands upon the receptiveness of the spectator. In order to reward the audience for its efforts, Fassbinder throws out several not-too-subtle jokes; the six parts of the comedy are bound together by intertitles, grafitti from West Berlin toilets, precisely localized and dated, and witticisms and obscenities which have the same air of impudence as the rest of the film. No wonder then that Fassbinder had to produce the film by himself, that the Westdeutscher Rundfunk didn't want to collaborate on it, that the Berlin Senate extended no credit. As a result, we have something that seldom occurs in the Bundesrepublik—the independent film of an independent man.

1. From *Frankfurter Rundschau,* Dec. 2, 1978, Supplement "Zeit und Bild", p. 3.
2. Interview in *Frankfurter Rundschau,* Feb. 20, 1979, p. 12.

Berlin Alexanderplatz (1980)

Berlin, 1927. Franz Biberkopf (Gunter Lamprecht), a sometime transportation worker and pimp, is a familiar and popular figure with the poor workers and petty criminals in the Alexanderplatz district where he hangs out. Although good-natured and generous, Franz has an uncontrollable temper which has gotten him into trouble more than once. He has just been released after spending four years in prison for killing his mistress, Ida (Barbara Valentin), in a jealous rage. Now, he hopes to make a new life for himself, to get a good job—to become "respectable". However, there is a Depression, and work is hard to come by. Influenced by Reinhold (Gottfried John), a streetwise hustler for whom Franz feels an almost compulsory affinity, he strays again from the straight and narrow. Reinhold introduces him to Pum, the boss of a gang of thieves, and during a "job,"

Berlin Alexanderplatz

Franz is run over by an automobile and loses his right arm. Still undaunted, he is determined to make a decent life for himself and his new girlfriend Mieze (Barbara Sukowa), a warmhearted, rather naive young prostitute from the provinces, who continues working against his wishes to help make ends meet. The two have fun together; they share the same dreams; he calls her his "most beloved in all the world." Reinhold is also attracted to Mieze, but when she rejects his advances, he kidnaps and murders her. This is the last straw for Franz. That the man he considered to be his best friend should do such a thing to the only woman he ever really loved is incomprehensible to him. For all his failings, Franz had believed in the basic goodness of humanity. He cracks up. In a mental hospital, he learns that he must become a "useful member of society." When he is released, he takes a menial job in a factory. Franz Biberkopf has finally grown up.

For an analysis of the film, see Wolfram Schutte's article.

Lili Marleen (1981)

Willie Bunterberg (Hanna Schygulla), a young German singer working in a cabaret in Zurich, and Robert Mendelsson (Giancarlo Giannini), an aspiring classical musician from a wealthy Jewish family, are in love and plan to marry. The time is 1938. However, Robert's father David (Mel Ferrer), leader of an underground group dedicated to helping Jews and other political refugees to escape from Germany, considers Willie a liability, and arranges for her deportation from Switzerland. Although Robert really loves Willie, he feels he must continue his work in his father's organization, and knows that any open association with her in Germany would be as dangerous for her as for himself. He must give her up for the time being.

Looking for work, Willie visits Henkel (Karl Heinz von Hassel), a Nazi bureaucrat she met in Zurich. He has become an official in the Culture Ministry, and arranges for her to make a recording of a simple sailor's song, "Lili Marleen," which tells of a woman who waits faithfully for her lover to return. When the song is played by chance over a military radio network, the German troops respond overwhelmingly, and Willie and her accompanist Taschner (Hark Bohm) become overnight celebrities. Even Hitler is enchanted with the song (though Goebbels thinks it inappropriate to the Party line), and Willie is welcome in the highest Nazi circles. Robert's associates, whom she had met when she accompanied him on a trip to Germany, now seek to enlist her help. While on a tour to entertain the troops, she is approached by the leader of the Jewish underground, Gunther Weisenborn (Fassbinder), who asks her to smuggle film footage to the Allies. She agrees, using her privileged position to escape suspicion, and finally, to keep a rendezvous with Robert. A jealous fellow performer informs on her, and she is followed. Robert is taken into custody. Although they are not aware of his real identity, the Nazis torture him by isolating him in a room in which the song "Lili Marleen" is played over and over again. Then they arrange a monitored meeting between Willie and Robert, who manage to avoid allowing their relationship and activities to become evident to their captors.

Eventually, a deal is made with the underground whereby Robert and other political prisoners are exchanged at the Swiss border for the film footage Willie smuggled out. Although Willie's underground activities are never discovered, she is now considered "unreliable" and falls from grace. Taschner is sent to the Russian Front, where he is killed. Goebbels has "Lili Marleen" banned from the airwaves. Safe in Switzerland, Robert marries Miriam (Christine Kaufmann), a woman of his own religion and social class. Willie attempts suicide, but ends up in a hospital. In the meantime, the underground, grateful for her services and worried about her safety, manage to intervene into German military radio transmissions with the news of "Lili Marleen's" death in a concentration camp. Thousands of German fighting men are outraged, and the Party is forced to "rehabilitate" her. Suddenly, flowers from Goebbels appear at Willie's bedside. The story of her death is denounced as "hateful Jewish propaganda." At a huge outdoor rally reminiscent of Nuremburg, backed by a huge swastika, a glittering Willie sings her song again to assembled Nazis and to a radio audience of millions.

After the war, Willie returns to Zurich, hoping to take up where she left off with Robert. She arrives in time for a concert he is conducting at the opera house, and comes face to face with his wife. When he comes backstage, he sees her, but turns back to his audience to take his bows. As far as Willie is concerned he has made his choice, and she turns and leaves the theatre, and his life, forever.

Lili Marleen is Fassbinder's most expensive film to date (10.5 million DM). It is also, along with *Despair,* his most "international." It was originally shot in English, but both the German and American distributors eventually thought better of it, and it was re-dubbed into German. There is no question that Fassbinder intended to reach a mass audience with the film; it is big, colorful, and "easy"—in the tradition of *The Marriage of Maria Braun.* The film met with poor critical reception in Germany, where some suggested that the world's most prolific filmmaker was becoming "tired," while others found similarities to Lina Wertmuller's cynical, superficial *Seven Beauties.* Fassbinder has been called "tired" before, and has always bounced back. Although there is a sense, here, that the director bit off more than he could chew, there are rewards. The film is absolutely beautiful. Xaver Scharzenberger proves a worthy successor to Michael Ballhaus, and light and shadow have never been handled more expertly in a color film. Peer Raben's score, which works around the familiar title song with strains of Mahler which come to a crescendo in the last sequence, is totally effective. Fassbinder puts together a playful dictionary of his own favorite stylistic devices, while striving again toward the kind of naive melodrama he admires in Sirk's films. It works (the early love and farewell scenes with Robert, the death of the Hark Bohm character) as often as it doesn't (the "war" scenes, the final sequence).

The story itself, based upon Lale Andersen's autobiography *Der Himmel hat viele Farben (The Sky Has Many Colors)*, tells of a woman who is a survivor. Like Maria Braun, she is apolitical, practical, and basically only concerned with her love for Robert. She sings for the Nazis for the same reason she helps the underground—it seems "right" to her. Like other Fassbinder characters, she is deluded by love. It is implied that for all Robert's heroism, he is still a member of the upper class, and behaves accordingly when he marries the woman his father has chosen for him. He is a "realist", and becomes at the end what he would probably have become much sooner if the war had not intervened. Willie is cast adrift.

Lili Marleen is not a moving film, in spite of Hanna Schygulla's powerful performance. Hark Bohm, as the wisecracking, level-headed accompanist who doesn't want to go to war and may be gay and/or in love with Willie, is the most engaging character in the film. Giancarlo Giannini, in an uncharacteristically subdued role, is colorless, as may have been intended. Near the end of the film, a friendly Nazi officer escorts Willie through a forest to the Swiss border, and Fassbinder can't resist an "in" reference: he tells her that in the 1920s, a pimp murdered a prostitute there, and that a "poet" wrote a book about it. The set is the same that Fassbinder used for the murder scene in *Berlin Alexanderplatz*.

If Lili Marleen is not one of Fassbinder's best films, it may be seen as an attempt to come to grips with the problems raised in the making of "big" films for Fassbinder. It brings him, perhaps, one step closer to his dream of making "critical" Hollywood films in the tradition of Sirk, Walsh and Hitchcock, and, although not totally engaging, it has a warmth, a good-natured quality, which is rare in the work of this most negative of artists.

Video Productions

The Coffee House. 1970

Fassbinder's first studio production cannot be seen today. It is based on Fassbinder's and Peer Raben's Bremen production, but also contains elements of a later staging by the Munich anti-teater. Even the casting is a combination of the two productions. Botho Strauss wrote about the Bremen premiere in *Theater heute,* October, 1969, p. 16ff:

"Fassbinder has completely altered the dramatic style of Goldoni's *The Coffee House,* which pictures a concrete social locale in which a useless clique of early Italian bourgeois types alternate between games of love and money and are perceived as totally identical with the mechanics of comedy, intrigue, skulduggery and usury; that is, he has not interpreted or shown, has not followed, in this 'modernized' version, what was written in the original. This style is, compared to expectations one might have about a Goldoni comedy, actually a counter-style; lively verbal duels, all kinds of odd witticisms, and plays on words are sacrificed here to a more restrained and serenely spoken dialogue, and when it becomes insidious, it sounds especially elegiac. It is not even a comedy any more, but becomes a really very sad play.

Fassbinder read the original play thoroughly once, in order to commit the most important plot connections and characters to memory, but then wrote down what inspired him in the speeches in a freer form. So, this has become a totally new play, which can't be fruitfully compared with the older one."

Bremer Freiheit. 1972

Bremen in the early 19th century. Geesche (Margit Carstensen), a young wife, poisons her husband because he tyrannizes her. She even poisons her mother (Lilo Pempeit); she can no longer endure her reproaches about her immoral way of life. She kills her children because their bawling drives every man away. She finishes off her lover, by whom she is pregnant, on their wedding day. The grotesque wedding ceremony takes place as the poison she gave him already begins to take effect. Now one murder follows another until her ninth victim, a friend of her husband, informs the police.

Bremer Freiheit is based on an authentic event in the history of the city of Bremen. A townswoman, Geesche Gottfried, murdered fifteen people in the course of several years, but still enjoyed a reputation as a respectable, godfearing woman, because the poisonings were never recognized as such. Finally unmasked in 1831, she was beheaded in the last public execution in Bremen.

Fassbinder is not interested in the crime itself. Of course, he shows how the poison is administered (in almost ritualistic scenes, with piano music in the background), but only twice the direct result, the death. We are also spared the execution of Geesche. Fassbinder is only interested in the motive for the murders. In the first scene, the tone is already set: Miltenberger, always in closeup, calls for his newspaper, demands coffee, goes into a rage about the children's yelling, wants a drink. Intermittently, also in closeup, we see Geesche's feet, going back and forth again and again. This pattern is repeated throughout the play, varying and increasing. The men are always ordering Geesche about, even when it comes to sex. They regard Geesche as a piece of property. Geesche, who decides to stake a claim to her own free will, her own thoughts, her own happiness, in this male-dominated society, cannot accomplish her aim through love and understanding, but only through murder, which in the long run is no victory, but a capitulation, an act of desperation. At the end of this course there is no independence, but only loneliness.

Fassbinder took over and further developed elements from

the Bremen production of the play, which Wilfried Minks had designed. In Bremen, Geesche's dwelling was "a cross, swimming in a sea of thick blood, into which the expensive furniture half-threatens to sink. The stage, which we look down upon as upon an operating table, is surrounded at the sides by those freedom-cliches of the open sea: seagulls in a blue sky." (Hellmuth Karasek, *Theater heute*, 1/1972) In the white, almost empty playing space of the television studio, only one piece of furniture stands, like an island. Images are projected onto the back wall: the ocean in motion or totally quiet, ships, but also backwaters or huge, threatening rushes. The actors play their roles unpsychologically, like marionettes. Thus, Fassbinder has not shifted his morality tale back into the reality from which he abstracted it, but keeps it in the realm of theatrical stylization.

Nora Helmer. 1973

In order to finance a sojourn in Italy for her ailing husband Torvald (Joachim Hansen), Nora Helmer (Margit Carstensen) once borrowed money, by forging her father's name, from Krogstad (Ulli Lommel), a man who had passed bad checks and become involved in shady business dealings. Since then, Torvald has become director of the bank where Krogstad is now employed, and wants to dismiss him because of his past. Krogstad blackmails Nora, warning her that he will tell Torvald about their earlier dealings. Nora unsuccessfully tries to convince her husband to retain Krogstad. When Torvald learns the truth about his wife through a letter from Krogstad, he wants to divorce her, because he believes she has endangered his career. A second letter from Krogstad denies the charges, and Torvald decides he wants his wife back. But now, Nora doesn't accept his generosity. She leaves her husband, because he doesn't love her, because he didn't understand the motives for her behavior, and because he wasn't ready to accept any of the guilt for what happened.

Like *Martha* and *Effi Briest*, films that originate from approximately the same period, Fassbinder's adaptation of Ibsen's play also concerns a marriage in which the husband shows hardly any love for his wife, but wants to train her. While in the other two films the wife loses her battle with the husband, here she wins, even if she pays a heavy price for her victory. Although *Nora Helmer* is certainly related to other works of Fassbinder, it seems to me that his interest in the material, and the amount of intensive work invested, are much less than with *Martha* and *Effi Briest*. In the first place, Fassbinder was apparently so fascinated with the possibilities offered by a studio production in which there were five electronic cameras at his disposal, that his interest in the story itself was almost forgotten. The characters move like marionettes in a sepia-tinted hall of mirrors. Numerous subtle overexposures heighten the impact of the mirror images and shadows of the characters, who recite in uniform cadences texts which at one time Ibsen had used with great disruptive force .

In order to escape the optical-accoustical monotony Fassbinder at times avails himself, on the other hand, of certain strong moments that totally cancel out Ibsen's play. Krogstad, the blackmailer, must embrace Nora, as they had done earlier; Nora must remain cool and detatched from the beginning; thereby, the dramatic trajectory of the play falls apart.

Note: This filmography is not homogeneous; it is a work-in-progress, in which each of the individual descriptions of films is relevant, in principle, only from the standpoint of time in which it was originally published. These descriptions have not been altered or polished, so that the interpretations contain references to earlier films, but no anticipations of later ones. The articles on Eight Hours Are Not a Day *and* Niklashauser Fart *are by Wilfried Wiegand; those on* Berlin Alexanderplatz *and* Lili Marleen *are by Ruth McCormick.*

Documentation

By Hans Helmut Prinzler

Biography

Rainer Werner Fassbinder was born on May 31, 1946 in the
Bavarian town of Bad Worishofen. His father, Hellmuth
Fassbinder, was a doctor, and his mother, Liselotte, a
translator. He was educated at the Rudolf Steiner School and
at secondary schools in Augsberg and Munich. When his
parents separated, he stayed with his mother, who often sent
her son to the cinema in order to be able to work in peace at
home. Liselotte Eder now often appears in her son's films as
an actress under the name Lilo Pempeit. He left school
before graduation in 1964 and took various odd jobs, finally
studying drama at the Fridl-Leonhard Studio in Munich. In
mid-1967 he joined a group called Action-Theater: a "basement theatre" on Munich's Mullerstrasse. First he worked as
an actor, then as a director, then adapting plays, and finally,
writing his own works. His first, *Katzelmacher,* premiered at
the Action-Theater in April, 1968. Action-Theater was closed
by the police in May, 1968. Ten members of the group,
among them Fassbinder, Peer Raben, Hanna Schygulla,
Rudolf Waldemar Brem and Kurt Raab, went on to found
anti-teater, which played first at the "Buchner-Theater,"
then at the Academy of Art, and finally in the back room of
the Witwe Bolte, a Schwabing tavern, from late 1968 to late
1969. Then *anti-teater* lost its base, and went into "exile."
Fassbinder had already begun to work with his group in
films.

Fassbinder had made two short films in 1965-66 with the
collaboration of Christoph Roser, *Der Stadtstreicher* and
Das Kleine Chaos. In 1968, the *anti-teater ensemble* appeared
in Jean-Marie Straub's film, *The Bridegroom, the Actress
and the Pimp.*

In April, 1969 Fassbinder and his team made their first

full-length feature, *Love Is Colder than Death,* which received a cool reception at the Berlin Film Festival in June. With the next film, *Katzelmacher,* came the breakthrough: made in August, 1969, the film was shown at the Mannheim Festival in October, where it won the Film Critics' Prize, the Prize of the German Academy for Outstanding Artistic Achievement, and eventually, five prizes in all. On November 1, 1969, theater and film critics attended a "Rainer Werner Fassbinder Showdown" in Bremen, in which two films *(Love Is Colder than Death* and *Katzelmacher)* and two plays *(The Coffee House and Anarchy in Bavaria)* were shown.

Following is a balance sheet of Fassbinder's activities to date:

1969: 3 plays (written), 2 adaptations, 4 plays (directed), 4 films.

1970: 1 theatrical adaptation, 6 films, 2 radio plays, 1 television play.

1971: 3 plays (written), 3 plays (directed), 1 film, 1 radio play.

1972: 1 play (directed), 2 films, 1 television series (in 5 parts), 1 radio play, 1 television sketch.

1973: 2 plays (directed), 4 films (one in 2 parts), 1 television play (directed).

1974: 3 plays (directed), 1 film, 1 television show.

1975: 1 play (written and directed), 3 films.

1976: 3 films (one in 2 parts), 1 play (directed).

1977: 1 television play, 1 film, 1 episode in a film.

1978: 2 films.

1979-80: 2 films, 1 television series (in 14 parts).

(This list does not include Fassbinder's work as an actor, producer, theatre manager, composer, designer, editor and cameraman.)

Fassbinder has won State film prizes for *Katzelmacher* (1969), *Why Does Herr R Run Amok?* (1971), *Merchant of the Four Seasons* (1972), *Despair* (1978) and *The Marriage of Maria Braun* (1979).

In 1970 Fassbinder married the singer and anti-teater actress Ingrid Caven, and though they have since divorced, she appears regularly in his productions. In 1972 he participated in the founding of the Filmverlag der Autoren, and at the end of 1976 became a stockholder (with a 6.5% share) in the distribution company, which Rudolf Augstein saved from financial ruin. However, in mid-1977, Fassbinder terminated his association with the Filmverlag.

In 1971 Fassbinder also founded the production company Tango Films, which has since produced all of Fassbinder's independent films, as well as *The Tenderness of Wolves* (by Ulli Lommel) and *Morgen wirst du um mich weinen* (by Christian Hohoff). In the beginning of the 1974-75 season, Fassbinder took over the direction of the Frankfurt Theater am Turm (TAT); he resigned in June, 1975. He made the headlines in early 1976 with his play *Der Mull, die Stadt und der Tod (Garbage, the City and Death)*, because of its alleged antisemitism; conservative critics called him a "left wing fascist," and Suhrkamp Verlag withdrew its publication of the play. The play was later made into a film, *Shadows of Angels* by the Swiss director Daniel Schmid, which played in a few theatres in 1976 without incident. Fassbinder's plans to film two novels, *Die Erde ist unbewohnbar wie der Mond (The Earth is as Uninhabitable as the Moon)* by Gerhard Zwerenz and *Soll und Haben (Debit and Credit)* by Gustav Freytag, ran aground, because the Project Commission for Film Financing and the Director of the Westdeutschen Rundfunk rejected the two projects on the grounds that they contained material that could also be construed as anti-semitic.

Fassbinder has still not published a novel he had planned to finish in 1976. In the Summer of 1977 he announced that he planned to leave Germany to work in Hollywood. He collaborated on the film *Germany in Autumn* at the end of the year, and since then has completed four more films and a monumental 14-part television series, *Berlin Alexanderplatz*—all in Germany. He is currently finishing *Lola*, a remake of *The Blue Angel*.

Fassbinder has lived in West Berlin since the end of 1978.

Radio Plays

1970: *Preparadise Sorry Now* (Suddeutsche Rundfunk); *Ganz in Weiss* (Bayerischer Rundfunk).

1971: *Iphegenia on Tauris* by Johann Wolfgang Goethe (Westdeutscher Rundfunk).
1972: *Keiner ist bose und Keiner ist Gut* (Bayerischer Rundfunk).

Roles in Film and Television

1965: *Der Stadtstreicher* (man in pissoir).
1966: *Das Kleine Chaos* (one of the three "gangsters").
1967: *Tony's Freunde* (Mallard/dir. Paul Vasil).
1968: *The Bridegroom, the Actress and the Pimp* (Freder the Pimp/dir. Jean-Marie Straub).
1969: *Alarm* (man in uniform/dir. Dieter Lemmel), *Al Capone in Deutschen Wald* (Heini/dir. Franz Peter Wirth), *Baal* (Baal/dir. Volker Schlondorff), *Frei bis zum Nachsten Mal* (mechanic/dir. Korbinian Koberle), *Gods of the Plague* (porn dealer), *Katzelmacher* (Jorgos), *Love Is Colder than Death* (Franz).
1970: *The American Soldier* (Franz), *Matthias Kneissl* (Flecklbauer /dir. Reinhard Hauff), *Die Niklashauser Fahrt* (The Black Monk), *The Sudden Wealth of the Poor People of Kolmbach* (peasant/dir. Volker Schlondorff), *Rio das Mortes* (man who dances with Hanna Schygulla), *Supergirl* (man peeking through window/dir. Rudolf Thome), *Beware of a Holy Whore* (Sascha, Head of Production), *Whity* (guest in saloon).
1971: *Merchant of the Four Seasons* (Zucker).
1972: *Bremer Freiheit* (Rumpf).
1973: *Fear Eats the Soul* (Edgar), *Tenderness of Wolves* (Wittkowski /dir. Ulli Lommel).
1974: *1 Berlin Harlem* (himself/dir. Lothar Lambert), *Fox and His Friends* (Franz Biberkopf).
1975: *Shadows of Angels* (Raoul/dir. Daniel Schmid).
1976: *Adolf und Marlene* (Hermann/dir. Ulli Lommel).
1977: *Germany in Autumn* (himself), Der Kleine Godard (himself/dir. Hellmuth Costard).
1978: *The Marriage of Maria Braun* (black marketeer), *Bourbon Street Blues* (author/ group production of the Academy of Television and Film Studies, Munich, under the

direction of Douglas Sirk, Hans Schonherr and Tilman Taube).

1980: *Berlin Alexanderplatz* (himself in dream sequence), *Lili Marleen* (Gunther Weisenborn).

Plays, Adaptations and Productions

Title	Author	First Produced
Leonce and Lena	Buchner	Oct. 1967
Die Verbrecher	Bruckner	Dec. 1967
Zum Beispiel Ingolstadt	Fleisser/RWF	Feb. 1968
Katzelmacher	RWF	Apr. 1968
Axel Caesar Haarmann	Collective	Apr. 1968
Mockinpott	Weiss	July 1968
Orgie Ubuh	Jarry/RWF/Raben	Aug. 1968
Iphegenia on Tauris	Goethe/RWF	Oct. 1968
Ajax	Sophocles/RWF	Dec. 1968
American Soldier	RWF	Dec. 1968
Beggar's Opera	Gay/RWF	Feb. 1969
Pre-Paradise Sorry Now	RWF	Mar. 1969
Anarchy in Bavaria	RWF	June 1969
The Coffee House	Goldoni/RWF	Sept. 1969
Werewolf	Baer/RWF	Dec. 1969
The Burning Village	de Vega/RWF	Nov. 1970
Pioneers in Ingolstadt	Fleisser/RWF	Jan. 1971
Blood on the Cat's Collar	RWF	Mar. 1971
Petra von Kant	RWF	June 1971
Bremer Freiheit	RWF	Dec. 1971
Liliom	Molnar	Dec. 1972
Bibi	Heinrich Mann	Jan. 1973
Hedda Gabler	Ibsen	Dec. 1973
Die Unvernunftigen Sterben Aus	Handke	May 1974
Germinal	Zola/Karsunke	Sept. 1974
Uncle Vanya	Chekov	Dec. 1974
Der Mull, der Stadt und die Tod	RWF	Cancelled
Women in New York	Boothe	Sept. 1976

Filmography

Der Stadstreicher   (1965)

Screenplay	Rainer Werner Fassbinder
Camera Operator	Josef Jung
Production	Roser-Film

Cast: Christoph Roser, Susanne Schimkus, Michael Fengler, Thomas Fengler, Irm Hermann, Rainer Werner Fassbinder.

Running time, 10 mins.; 16 mm, B&W.

Das Kleine Chaos   (1966)

Screenplay	Rainer Werner Fassbinder
Camera Operator	Michael Fengler
Production	Roser-Film

Cast: Marite Grieselis, Christoph Roser, Lilo Pempeit, Greta Rehfeld, Rainer Werner Fassbinder.

Running time, 12 mins.; 35 mm, B&W.

Love Is Colder Than Death   (1969)
(Liebe Ist Kalter Als Der Tod)

For Claude Chabrol, Eric Rohmer, Jean-Marie Straub, Lino und Cuncho.

Screenplay	Rainer Werner Fassbinder
Camera Operator	Dietrich Lohmann
Editor	Franz Walsch
Music	Peer Raben, Holger Munzer
Set Design	Ulli Lommel, Rainer Werner Fassbinder
Assistant Director	(for several days) Martin Muller
Production	Anti-teater-X-Film

Cast: Ulli Lommel (Bruno), Hanna Schygulla (Joanna), Rainer Werner Fassbinder (Franz), Hans Hirschmuller (Peter), Katrin Schaake (woman in march), Peter Berling (arms dealer), Hannes Gromball (Joanna's customer), Gisela Otto (first prostitute), Ingrid Caven (second prostitute), Ursala Stratz (fat prostitute), Irm Herman (salesgirl), Les Olvides (Georges), Wil Rabenbauer (Jurgen), Peter Moland (judge at Syndicate trial), Anastassios Karalas (Turk), Rudolf Waldemar Brem (motorcycle cop), Yaak Karsunke (Commissioner of Police), Monika Stadler (young girl), Kurt Raab (department store detective).

Filmed in 24 days on location in Munich and surroundings in April, 1969.
Running time, 88 mins.; 35 mm, B&W.
Cost: 95,000 DM.

Katzelmacher (1969)

For Marie Luise Fleisser.
Motto: It is better to make new mistakes than to add to the universal lack of consciousness with old ones. (Yaak Karsunke).

Screenplay	Rainer Werner Fassbinder
Camera Operator	Dietrich Lohmann
Editor	Franz Walsch
Music	Peer Raben (after Franz Schubert).
Set Design	Rainer Werner Fassbinder
Assistant Director	Michael Fengler
Production	Antiteater-X-Film

Cast: Hanna Schygulla (Marie), Lilith Ungerer (Helga), Elga Sorbas (Rosy), Doris Mattes (Gunda), Rainer Werner Fassbinder (Jorgos), Rudolf Waldemar Brem (Paul), Hans Hirschmuller (Erich), Harry Baer (Franz), Peter Moland (Peter), Hannes Gromball (Klaus), Irm Hermann (Elisabeth), guest star: Katrin Schaake (woman on Landstrasse).

Filmed in 9 days on location in Munich in August, 1969.
Running time, 88 mins.; 35 mm, B&W.
Cost: 80,000 DM.
Distributed in the U.S. by New Yorker Films.

Far Jamaica (1969)
(Fernes Jamaica)

Director	Petér Moland
Screenplay	Rainer Werner Fassbinder
Camera Operator	Herbert Paetzold
Production	Antiteater

Cast: Katrin Schaake, Ulli Lommel, Hannes Gromball, Ingrid Caven, William Powell.

Running time, 14 mins.; 35 mm, widescreen, B&W.

Gods of the Plague (1969)
(Gotter der Pest)

Screenplay	Rainer Werner Fassbinder
Camera Operator	Dietrich Lohmann
Editor	Franz Walsch
Music	Peer Raben
Set Design	Kurt Raab
Assistant Director	Kurt Raab
Production	Antiteater
With the collaboration of	Michael Fengler

Cast: Harry Baer (Franz), Hanna Schygulla (Joanna), Margarethe von Trotta (Margarethe), Gunther Kaufmann (Gunther), Carla Aulaulu (Carla), Ingrid Caven (Magdalena Fuller), Jan George (cop), Marian Seidowski (Marian), Yaak Karsunke (Commissioner), Micha Cochina (Joe), Hannes Gromball (supermarket manager), Lilith Ungerer (woman in cafe), Katrin Schaake (owner of cafe), Lilo Pempeit (Mother), Rainer Werner Fassbinder (porno dealer), Irm Hermann, Peter Molan, Doris Mattes.

Filmed in 3 weeks on location in Munich, Dingolfing in October and November, 1969.
Running time, 91 mins.; 35 mm, B&W.
Cost: 180,000 DM.
Distributed in the U.S. by New Yorker Films.

Why Does Herr R Run Amok?   (1969)
(Warum lauft Herr R amok?)

Screenplay	Improvisations by Michael Fengler/ Rainer Werner Fassbinder
Camera Operator	Dietrich Lohmann
Editor	Franz Walsch, Michael Fengler
Music	Christian Anders
Set Design	Kurt Raab
Assistant Director	Harry Baer
Production	Antiteater, produced by Maran-Film in collaboration with the Suddeutscher Rundfunk

Cast: Kurt Raab (Herr R), Lilith Ungerer (his wife), Amadeus Fengler (their son), Franz Maron (boss), Harry Baer/Peter Moland/Lilo Pempeit (colleagues in office), Hanna Schygulla (school friend), Herr and Frau Steer (father and mother), Peer Raben (school friend), Carla Aulaulu/Eva Pampuch (record salesgirls), Ingrid Caven/Doris Mattes/Irm Hermann/ Hannes Gromball (neighbors), Peter Hamm/Jochen Pinkert (policemen), Eva Madelung (boss's sister).

Filmed in 13 days in Munich in December, 1969.
Running time, 88 mins.; 16 mm, enlarged to 35 mm, color.
Cost: 135,000 DM.
Distributed in the U.S. by New Yorker Films.

Rio Das Mortes   (1970)

Screenplay	Rainer Werner Fassbinder (from an idea by Volker Schlondorff)
Camera Operator	Dietrich Lohmann
Editor	Thea Eymesz
Music	Peer Raben
Set Design	Kurt Raab
Assistant Director	Harry Baer, Kurt Raab
Production	Janus Film und Fernsehen/Antiteater-X-Film

Cast: Hanna Schygulla (Hanna), Michael Konig (Michel), Gunther Kaufmann (Gunther), Katrin Schaake (Katrin, Hanna's friend), Joachim von Mengershausen (Katrins boyfriend), Lilo Pempeit (Gunther's mother), Franz Maron (Hanna's uncle), Harry Baer (Michel's colleague), Marius Aicher (boss), Carla Aulaulu (customer), Walter Sedlmayr (secretary), Ulli Lommel (automobile dealer), Monika Stadler (employee in travel bureau),

The Coffee House   (1970)
(Das Kaffeehaus)

Adaption by R. W. Fassbinder and the Munich anti-teater under the direction of Peer Raben and R. W. Fassbinder, developed for and played by the Bremer Ensemble.

Screenplay	Rainer Werner Fassbinder (from Carlo Goldoni's play)
Camera Operator	Dietbert Schmidt, Manfred Forster
Music	Peer Raben
Set Design	Wilfried Minks
Production	Westdeutscher Rundfunk

Cast: Margit Carstensen (Vittoria), Ingrid Caven (Placida), Hanna Schygulla (Lisaura), Kurt Raab (Don Marzio), Harry Baer (Eugenio), Hans Hirschmuller (Trappolo), Gunther Kaufmann (Leander), Peter Moland (Pandolfo), Wil Rabenbauer (Ridolfo).

Filmed in 10 days in Cologne (Studio) in February, 1970.
Running time, 105 mins.; B&W.

Whity   (1970)

For Peter Berling.

Screenplay	Rainer Werner Fassbinder
Camera Operator	Michael Ballhaus
Editor	Franz Walsch, Thea Eymesz
Music	Peer Raben
Set Design	Kurt Raab
Assistant Director	Harry Baer
Production	Atlantis Film/Antiteater-X-Film

Cast: Gunther Kaufmann (Whity), Hanna Schygulla (Hanna), Ulli Lommel (Frank), Harry Baer (Davy), Katrin Schaake (Katherine), Ron Randell (Mr. Nicholson), Thomas Blanco (Mexican quack), Stefano Capriati (lawyer), Elaine Baker (Whity's mother), Mark Salvage (Sheriff), Helga Ballhaus (lawyer's wife), Kurt Raab (pianist), Rainer Werner Fassbinder (man in saloon).

Filmed in 20 days on location in Almeria, Spain in April, 1970.
Running time, 95 mins.; 35 mm, Cinemascope, color.
Cost: 680,000 DM.

Die Niklashauser Fart (1970)

Screenplay	Rainer Werner Fassbinder/Michael Fengler
Camera Operator	Dietrich Lohmann
Editor	Thea Eymesz, Franz Walsch
Music	Peer Raben, Amon Duul II
Set Design	Kurt Raab
Assistant Director	Harry Baer
Production	Janus Film und Fernsehen (for Westdeutscher Rundfunk)

Cast: Michael Konig (Hans Bohm), Michael Gordon (Antonio), Rainer Werner Fassbinder (Black Monk), Hanna Schygulla (Johanna), Walter Sedlmayr (priest), Margit Carstensen (Margarethe), Franz Maron (her husband), Kurt Raab (Bishop), Gunther Rupp (his councelor), Karl Scheydt (townsman), Gunther Kaufmann (leader of peasants), Siggi Graue (first peasant), Michael Fengler (second peasant), Ingrid Caven (screaming woman), Elga Sorbas (fainting woman), Carla Aulaulu (epileptic woman), Peer Raben (Monsignor), Peter Berling (executioner), Magdalena Montezuma (Penthesilea).

Filmed in 20 days on location in Munich, Starnberg, Feldkirchen in May, 1970.
Running time, 86 mins.; 16 mm, color.
Cost: 550,000 DM.

The American Soldier (1970)
(Der Amerikanische Soldat)

Screenplay	Rainer Werner Fassbinder
Camera Operator	Dietrich Lohmann
Editor	Thea Eymesz
Music	Peer Raben; Song "So Much Tenderness" by Fassbinder/sung by Gunther Kaufmann
Set Design	Kurt Raab, Rainer Werner Fassbinder
Assistant Director	Kurt Raab
Production	Antiteater

Cast: Karl Scheydt (Ricky), Elga Sorbas (Rosa), Jan George (Jan), Margarethe von Trotta (chambermaid), Hark Bohm (Doc), Ingrid Caven (singer), Eva Ingeborg Scholz (Ricky's mother), Kurt Raab (Ricky's brother), Marius Aicher (policeman), Gustl Datz (police chief), Marquard

Bohm (private detective), Rainer Werner Fassbinder (Franz), Katrin Schaake (Magdalena Fuller), Ulli Lommel (gypsy), Irm Hermann (whore).

Filmed in 15 days in Munich in August, 1970.
Running time, 80 mins.; 35 mm, B&W.
Cost: 280,000 DM.
Distributed in the U.S. by New Yorker Films.

Beware of a Holy Whore   (1970)
(Warnung vor einer heiligen Nutte)

Motto: Pride comes before the fall.

Screenplay	Rainer Werner Fassbinder
Camera Operator	Michael Ballhaus
Editor	Franz Walsch, Thea Eymesz
Music	Peer Raben, Gaetano Donizetti, Elvis Presley, Ray Charles, Leonard Cohen, Spooky Tooth
Set Design	Kurt Raab
Assistant Director	Harry Baer
Production	Antiteater-X-Film/Nova International, Rome.

Cast: Lou Castel (Jeff, director), Eddie Constantine (himself), Hanna Schygulla (Hanna, actress), Marquard Bohm (Ricky, actor), Rainer Werner Fassbinder (Sascha, production manager), Ulli Lommel (Korbinian, producer), Katrin Schaake (scriptgirl), Benjamin Lev (Candy, producer), Monika Teuber (Billi, makeup woman), Margarethe von Trotta (production secretary), Gianni di Luigi (cameraman), Rudolf Waldemar Brem (director of lighting), Herb Andress (coach), Thomas Schieder (Jesus), Kurt Raab (Fred), Hannes Fuchs (David), Marcella Michelangeli (Margret), Ingrid Caven (extra), Harry Baer (her husband), Magdalena Montezuma (Irm), Werner Schroeter (Dieters, photographer), Karl Scheydt, Tanja Constatine, Maria Novelli, Enzo Monteduro, Achmed Em Bark, Michael Fengler, Burghard Schlicht, Dick Randall, Peter Berling, Tony Bianchi, Renato dei Laudadio, Gianni Javarone, Peter Gauhe, Marcello Zucche.

Filmed in 22 days on location in Sorrento, Italy in September, 1970.
Running time, 103 mins.; 35 mm, color.
Cost: 1,100,000 DM.
Distributed in the U.S. by New Yorker Films.

Pioneers in Ingolstadt   (1970)
(Pioniere in Ingolstadt)

Screenplay	Rainer Werner Fassbinder (from a play by Marie Luise Fleisser)
Camera Operator	Dietrich Lohmann
Editor	Thea Eymesz
Music	Peer Raben
Set Design	Kurt Raab
Assistant Director	Gunther Kraa
Production	Janus Film und Fernsehen/Antiteater (for Zweites Deutsches Fernsehen)

Cast: Hanna Schygulla (Berta), Harry Baer (Karl), Irm Hermann (Alma), Rudolf Waldemar Brem (Fabian), Walter Sedlmayr (Fritz), Klaus Lowitsch (sergeant-major), Gunther Kaufmann (Max), Carla Aulaulu (Frieda), Elga Sorbas (Mariel), Burghard Schlicht (Klaus), Gunther Kraa (Gottfried).

Filmed in 25 days on location in Landsberg-Lech, Munich in November, 1970. Running time, 83 mins., 35 mm, color. Cost: 550,000 DM.

Merchant of the Four Seasons   (1971)
(Der Handler der vier Jahrezeiten)

Screenplay	Rainer Werner Fassbinder
Camera Operator	Dietrich Lohmann
Editor	Thea Eymesz
Music	"Buona Notte" by Rocco Granata
Set Design	Kurt Raab
Assistant Director	Harry Baer
Production	Tango Film

Cast: Hans Hirschmuller (Hans Epp), Irm Hermann (his wife), Hanna Schygulla (his sister), Andrea Schober (his daughter), Gusti Kreissl (his mother), Kurt Raab (his brother-in-law), Heide Simon (his married sister), Klaus Lowitsch (Harry), Karl Scheydt (Anzell), Ingrid Caven (Hans' "great love"), Peter Chatel (doctor), Lilo Pempeit (customer), Walter Sedlmayr (seller of fruit cart), Salem El Hedi (Arab), Hark Bohm (policeman), Daniel Schmid/Harry Baer/Marian Seidowski (job applicants), Michael Fengler (playboy), Rainer Werner Fassbinder (Zucker), Elga Sorbas (Marile Kosemund).

Filmed in 11 days on location in Munich in August, 1971.
Running time, 89 mins.; 35 mm, color.
Cost: 178,000 DM.
Distributed in the U.S. by New Yorker Films.

The Bitter Tears of Petra von Kant   (1972)
(Die Bitteren Tranen der Petra von Kant)

Screenplay	Rainer Werner Fassbinder
Camera Operator	Michael Ballhaus
Editor	Thea Eymesz
Music	The Platters, The Walker Brothers, Guiseppe Verdi
Set Design	Kurt Raab
Assistant Director	Harry Baer, Kurt Raab
Production	Tango Film

Cast: Margit Carstensen (Petra von Kant), Hanna Schygulla (Karin Thimm), Irm Hermann (Marlene), Eva Mattes (Gabrielle von Kant), Katrin Schaake (Sidonie von Grasenabb), Gisela Fackeldey (Valerie von Kant).

Filmed in 10 days in Worpswede in January,1972.
Running time, 124 mins.; 35 mm, color.
Cost: 325,000 DM.
Distributed in the U.S. by New Yorker Films.

Jail Bait   (1972)
(Wildwechsel)

Screenplay	Rainer Werner Fassbinder (from the stage play by Franz Xaver Kroetz)
Camera Operator	Dietrich Lohmann
Editor	Thea Eymesz
Music	Ludwig van Beethoven
Set Design	Kurt Raab
Assistant Director	Irm Hermann
TV Adaptation	Rolf Defrank
Production	Intertel (for Sender Freies Berlin)

Cast: Jorg von Liebenfels (Erwin), Ruth Drexel (Hilda, his wife), Eva Mattes (Hanni, his daughter), Harry Baer (Franz), Rudolf Waldemar Brem (Dieter), Hanna Schygulla (doctor), Kurt Raab (boss), Karl Scheydt/Klaus Lowitsch (policeman), Irm Hermann/Marquard Bohm (prison guards), El Hedi Ben Salem (friend).

Filmed in 14 days on location in Straubing and environs in March, 1972.
Running time, 102 mins.; 35 mm, color.
Cost: 550,000 DM.
Distributed in the U.S. by New Yorker Films.

Eight Hours Are Not a Day   (1972)
(Acht Stunden sind kein Tag)

Screenplay	Rainer Werner Fassbinder
Camera Operator	Dietrich Lohmann
Editor	Marie Anne Gerhardt
Music	Jean Gepoint (= Jens Wilhelm Petersen)
Set Design	Kurt Raab
Assistant Director	Renate Leiffer, Eberhard Schubert
TV Adaptation	Peter Marthesheimer
Production	Westdeutscher Rundfunk

Cast: Gottfried John (Jochen), Hanna Schygulla (Marion), Luise Ulrich (Grandma), Werner Finck (Gregor), Anita Bucher (Kathe), Wolfried Lier (Wolf), Christine Oesterlein (Klara), Renate Roland (Monika), Kurt Raab (Harald), Andrea Schober (Sylvia), Thorsten Massinger (Manni), Irm Hermann (Irmgard Erlkonig), Wolfgang Zerlett (Manfred), Wolfgang Schenck (Franz), Herb Andress (Rudiger), Rudolf Waldemar Brem (Rolf), Hans Hirschmuller (Jurgen), Peter Gauhe (Ernst), Grigorios Karipidis (Giuseppe), Karl Scheydt (Peter), Victor Curland (Foreman Kretzschmer), Rainer Hauer (Floor Manager Gross), Margit Carstensen/Christiane Jannessen/Doris Mattes/Gusti Kreissl/Lilo Pempeit (housewives), Katrin Schaake/Rudolf Lenz/Jorg von Liebenfels (landlords), guests: Ulli Lommel, Ruth Drexel, Walter Sedlmayr, Helga Feddersen, Heinz Meier, Karl-Heinz Vosgerau, Peter Chatel, Valeska Gert, Eva Mattes, Marquard Bohm, Klaus Lowitsch, Hannes Gromball, Peter Marthesheimer.

Filmed in 105 days on location at the Monchen-Gladkach factory, Cologne, in April through August, 1972
Running time: Part I: 101 mins., 11 secs.; Part II: 99 mins., 31 secs.; Part III: 91 mins., 56 secs.; Part IV: 88 mins., 53 secs.; Part V: 88 mins., 53 secs.; 16mm, color.
Cost: 1,375,000 DM.

Bremen Freedom (1972)
(Bremer Freiheit)

Teleplay by Rainer Werner Fassbinder and Dietrich Lohmann, developed from Fassbinder's production with the Bremen Playhouse Ensemble.

Screenplay	Rainer Werner Fassbinder
Camera Operator	Dietrich Lohmann, Hans Schugg, Peter Weyrich
Editor	Friedrich Niquet, Monika Solzbacher
Set Design	Kurt Raab
Assistant Director	Fritz Muller-Scherz
TV Adaptation	Karlhans Reuss
Production	Telefilm Saar

Cast: Margit Carstensen (Geesche), Ulli Lommel (Miltenberger), Wolfgang Schenck (Gottfried), Walter Sedlmayr (clergyman), Wolfgang Kieling (Timm), Rodulf Waldemar Brem (cousin Bohm), Kurt Raab (Zimmermann), Fritz Schediwy (Johann), Hanna Schygulla (Luise Maurer), Rainer Werner Fassbinder (Rumpf), Lilo Pempeit (Mother).

Filmed in 9 days in Saarbrucken (studio) in September, 1972.
Running time, 87 mins.; color.
Cost: 240,000 DM.

World on Wires (1973)
(Welt am Draht)

Screenplay	Fritz Muller-Scherz/Rainer Werner Fassbinder (from a novel by Daniel F. Galouye)
Camera Operator	Michael Ballhaus
Editor	Marie Anne Gerhardt
Music	Gottfried Hungsberg/Archiv.
Set Design	Kurt Raab
Assistant Director	Renate Leiffer, Fritz Muller-Scherz
TV Adaptation	Peter Marthesheimer, Alexander Wesemann
Production	Westdeutscher Rundfunk

Cast: Klaus Lowitsch (Fred Stiller), Mascha Raaben (Eva), Adrian Hoven (Vollmer), Ivan Desny (Lause), Barbara Valentin (Gloria), Karl-Heinz Vosgerau (Siskins), Gunter Lamprecht (Wolfgang), Margit Carstensen (Schmidt-Gentner), Wolfgang Schenck (Hahn), Joachim Hansen

(Edelkern), Rudolf Lenz (Hartmann), Kurt Raab (Holm), Karl Scheydt (Lehner), Rainer Hauer (Stuhlfaut), Ulli Lommel (Rupp), Heinz Meier (Weinlaub), Peter Chatel (Hirse), guests: Ingrid Caven, Eddie Constantine, Gottfried John, Elma Karlowa, Christine Kaufmann, Rainer Langhans, Bruce Low, Karsten Peters, Katrin Schaake, Walter Sedlmayr, Elhedi Ben Salem, Christiane Maybach, Rudolf Waldemar Brem, Peter Kern, Ernst Kusters, Peter Moland, Doris Mattes, Liselotte Eder, Solange Pradel, Maryse Dellannoy, Werner Schroeter, Magdalena Montezuma, Corrina Brocher, Peter Gauhe, Dora Karras-Frank.

Filmed in 44 days in Cologne, Munich and Paris in January through March, 1973.
Running time, Part I: 99 mins., 25 secs.; Part II: 105 mins., 44 secs.; 16 mm, color.
Cost: 950,000 DM.

Nora Helmer   (1973)

Screenplay	Play by Henry Ibsen, translated by Bernhard Schulze
Camera Operators	Willi Raber, Wilfried Mier, Peter Weyrich, Gisela Loew, Hans Schugg
Editor	Anne-Marie Bornheimer, Friedrich Niquet
Set Design	Friedhelm Boehm
Assistant Director	Fritz Muller-Scherz, Rainer Langhans
Production	Telefilm Saar (for Saarlandischer Rundfunk)

Cast: Margit Carstensen (Nora), Joachim Hansen (Torvald), Barbara Valentin (Frau Linde), Ulli Lommel (Krogstedt), Klaus Lowitsch (Dr. Rank), Lilo Pempeit (Marie), Irm Hermann (Helene).

Filmed in 21 days in Saarbrucken (studio) in May, 1973.
Running time, 101 mins.; color.
Cost: 550,000 DM.

Fear Eats the Soul   (1973)
(Angst essen Seele auf)

Screenplay	Rainer Werner Fassbinder
Camera Operator	Jurgen Jurges
Editor	Thea Eymesz
Music	from Archives
Set Design	Rainer Werner Fassbinder
Assistant Director	Rainer Langhans
Production	Tango Film

Cast: Brigitte Mira (Emmi), El Hedi Ben Salem (Ali), Barbara Valentin (Barbara), Irm Hermann (Krista), Rainer Werner Fassbinder (Eugen), Karl Scheydt (Albert), Elma Karlowa (Frau Kargus), Anita Bucher (Frau Ellis), Gusti Kreissl (Paula), Walter Sedlmayr (grocer), Doris Mattes (his wife), Liselotte Eder (Frau Munchmeyer), Marquard Bohm (Gruber, landlord's son), Hannes Gromball (head waiter), Katharina Herbert, Rudolf Waldemar Brem, Peter Moland, Margit Symo , Peter Gauhe, Helga Ballhaus.

Filmed in 15 days on location in Munich in September, 1973.
Running time, 93 mins.; 35 mm, widescreen, color.
Cost: 260,000 DM.
Distributed in the U.S. by New Yorker Films.

Martha   (1973)

Screenplay	Rainer Werner Fassbinder
Camera Operator	Michael Ballhaus
Editor	Liesgret Schmitt-Klink
Music	from Archives
Set Design	Kurt Raab
Assistant Director	Fritz Muller-Scherz, Renate Leiffer
Production	Westdeutscher Rundfunk

Cast: Margit Carstensen (Martha Hyer/later: Martha Salomon), Karlheinz Bohm (Helmut Salomon), Gisela Fackeldey (mother), Adrian Hoven (Father), Barbara Valentin (Marianne), Ingrid Caven (Ilse), Ortrud Beginnen (Erna), Wolfgang Schenck (boss), Gunter Lamprecht (Dr. Salomon), Peter Chatel (Kaiser), Salem El Hedi (hotel guest), Kurt Raab (secretary in Embassy), Rudolf Lenz (porter).

Filmed in 25 days in Konstanz, Ottobeuren, Kreuzlingen, Rome in July through September, 1973.
Running time, 111 mins., 33 secs.; 16 mm, color.
Cost: 500,000 DM.

Effi Briest (1972-74)
(Fontane Effi Briest)

or Many Who Have a Notion of their Possibilities and their Needs still Accept the Prevailing Order by their Actions, and by Doing so, Strengthen and Confirm It.

Screenplay	Rainer Werner Fassbinder (from a novel by Fontane)
Camera Operator	Dietrich Lohmann, Jurgen Jurges
Editor	Thea Eymesz
Music	Camille Saint-Saens
Set Design	Kurt Raab
Assistant Director	Rainer Langhans, Fritz Muller-Scherz
Production	Tango Film

Cast: Hanna Schygulla (Effi), Wolfgang Schenck (Baron Geert von Innstetten), Karlheinz Bohm (Councellor Wullersdorf), Ulli Lommel (Major Crampas), Ursula Stratz (Roswitha), Irm Hermann (Johanna), Lilo Pempeit (Luise von Briest, Effi's mother), Herbert Steinmetz (Herr von Briest, Effi's father), Hark Bohm (Pharmacist Gieshubler), Rudolf Lenz (Councellor Rummschuttel), Barbara Valentin (Marietta Tripelli, singer), Karl Scheydt (Kruse), Theo Tecklenburg (Pastor Niemeyer), Barbara Lass (Polish cook), Eva Mattes (Hulda), Andrea Schober (Annie), Anndorthe Braker (Frau Pasche), Peter Gauhe (Cousin Dagobert).
Narrator: Rainer Werner Fassbinder.
Dubbed voices: Wolfgang Hess for Ulli Lommel, Kurt Raab for Hark Bohm, Renate Kuster for Ursula Stratz, Fred Maire for Herbert Steinmetz, Rosemarie Fendel for Lilo Pempeit, Margit Carstensen for Irm Hermann. Hanna Schygulla, Wolfgang Schenck and Karlheinz Bohm speak in their own voices.

Filmed in 58 days in Munich, Vienna, Aeroskobing (Denmark), Schleswig-Holstein (at Castle Bredeneek) and in the Black Forest (the railway trips) in September-October, 1972, October-November, 1973.
Running time, 141 mins.; 35 mm, B&W.
Cost: 750,000 DM.

Fox and His Friends   (1974)
(Faustrecht der Freiheit)

For Armin and all the others.

Screenplay	Rainer Werner Fassbinder
Camera Operator	Michael Ballhaus
Editor	Thea Eymesz
Music	Peer Raben Archives
Set Design	Kurt Raab
Assistant Director	Irm Hermann
Production	Tango Film/City Film GmbH, Berlin

Cast: Rainer Werner Fassbinder (Franz), Peter Chatel (Eugen), Karlheinz Bohm (Max), Rudolf Lenz (lawyer), Karl Scheydt (Klaus), Hans Zander (Springer), Kurt Raab (Vodka-Peter), Adrian Hoven (Eugen's father), Ulla Jacobsen (Eugen's mother), Irm Hermann (Madame Cherie), Kitty Buchhammer (Madame Isabell), Ursula Stratz (Madame Antoinette), Christiane Maybach (Franz's sister), Elma Karlowa, Harry Baer, Peter Kern, Barbara Valentin, Bruce Low, Walter Sedlmayr, El Hedi Ben Salem.

Filmed in 21 days on location in Marrakesch and Munich in April and July, 1974.
Running time, 123 mins.; 35 mm, color.
Cost: 450,000 DM.
Distributed in the U.S. by New Yorker Films.

Like a Bird on a Wire   (1974)
(Wie ein Vogel auf dem Draht)

Screenplay	Rainer Werner Fassbinder/Christian Hohoff; Lyrics: Anja Hauptmann
Camera Operator	Erhard Spandel
Musical Arranger	Ingfried Hoffmann; orchestra directed by Kurt Edelhagen
TV Adaptation	Rolf Spinrads
Set Design	Kurt Raab
Production	Westdeutscher Rundfunk

Cast: Brigitte Mira, Evelyn Kunnecke.

Filmed in 6 days in Cologne (studio) in July, 1974.
Running time, 44 mins.
Cost: 150,000 DM.

Mother Kusters Goes to Heaven   (1975)
(Mutter Kusters Fahrt zum Himmel)

Screenplay	Rainer Werner Fassbinder with the collaboration of Kurt Raab
Camera Operator	Michael Ballhaus
Editor	Thea Eymesz
Music	Peer Raben
Set Design	Kurt Raab
Assistant Director	Renate Leiffer
Production	Tango Film

Cast: Brigitte Mira (Mother Kusters), Ingrid Caven (Corinna), Karlheinz Bohm (Tillmann), Margit Carstensen (Frau Tillman), Irm Hermann (Helene), Gottfried John (Niemeyer), Armin Meier (Ernst) and Kurt Raab, Peter Kern, Peter Chatel, Vitus Zeplichal, Y Sa Lo, Lilo Pempeit and Matthias Fuchs.

Filmed in 20 days in Frankfurt am Main in February-March, 1975.
Running time, 120 mins.; 35 mm, color.
Cost: 750,000 DM.
Distributed in the U.S. by New Yorker Films.

Fear of Fear   (1975)
(Angst vor der Angst)

Screenplay	Rainer Werner Fassbinder from an idea by Asta Scheib
Camera Operator	Jurgen Jurges, Ulrich Prinz
Editor	Liesgret Schmitt-Klink, Beate Fischer-Weiskirch
Music	Peer Raben
Set Design	Kurt Raab
Production	Peter Marthesheimer; Westdeutscher Rundfunk.

Cast: Margit Carstensen (Margot), Ulrich Faulhaber (Kurt), Brigitte Mira (mother), Irm Hermann (Lore), Armin Meier (Karli), Adrian Hoven (Dr. Merck), Kurt Raab (Herr Bauer), Ingrid Caven (Edda), Lilo Pempeit (Frau Schall), Helga Marthesheimer (Frau Dr. von Unruh), Herbert Steinmetz (Dr. Auer), Hark Bohm (Dr. Rozenbaum), Constanze Haas (Bibi).

Filmed in 25 days in Cologne and Bonn in April-May, 1975.
Running time, 88 mins.; 16 mm, color.
Cost: 375,000 DM.

Shadows of Angels (1975)
(Schatten der Angel)

Director	Daniel Schmid
Screenplay	Daniel Schmid, Rainer Werner Fassbinder (from the play "Der Mull, die Stadt und der Tod")
Camera Operator	Renato Berta
Editor	Ila von Hasperg
Sound	Gunter Kortwich
Music	Peer Raben, Gottfried Hungsberg
Set Design	Raul Gimenez
Production	Albatros Produktion

Cast: Ingrid Caven (Lily Brest), Rainer Werner Fassbinder (Raoul), Klaus Lowitsch (Jew), Annemarie Duringer (Frau Muller), Adrian Hoven (Muller), Boy Gobert (Muller II), Ulli Lommel (Kleine Prinz), Jean-Claude Dreyfuss (Zwerg), Irm Hermann (Emma), Debria Kalpataru (Marie-Antionette), Hans Gratzer (Oscar), Peter Chatel (Mann, Thomas), Ila von Hasperg (Violet), Gail Curtis (Tau), Christine Jurku (Olga), Raul Gimenez (Jim), Alexander Allerson (Hans von Gluck), Harry Baer (Helfritz).

Filmed in 28 days in Vienna in October-November, 1975.
Running time, 101 mins.; 35 mm, color.
Cost: 600,000 DM.

I Only Want You to Love Me (1975/76)
(Ich will doch nur, dass Ihr mich liebt)

Screenplay	Rainer Werner Fassbinder (from a story in the book *Lebenslanglich* by Klaus Antes and Christiane Ehrhardt)
Camera Operator	Michael Ballhaus
Editor	Liesgret Schmitt-Klink
Music	Peer Raben
Set Design	Kurt Raab
Assistant Director	Renate Leiffer, Christian Hohoff
Production	Peter Marthesheimer; Bavaria Atelier GmbH (for Westdeutscher Rundfunk)

Cast: Vitus Zeplichal (Peter), Elke Aberle (Erika), Alexander Allerson (father), Ernie Mangold (mother), Johanna Hofer (grandmother), Katharina Buchhammer (Ulla), Wolfgang Hess (construction boss), Armin Meier (worker), Erika Runge (psychologist), Ulrich Radke (Erika's father), Annemarie Wendl (Erika's mother), Janos Gonczol (innkeeper), Edith Volkmann (innkeeper's wife), Robert Naegele, Axel Ganz, Inge Schulz, Heinz H. Bernstein, Helga Bender, Adi Gruber, Sonja Neubauer, Heide Ackermann, Reinhard Brex.

Filmed in 25 days in Munich and environs in November-December, 1975.
Running time, 103 mins.; 16 mm, color.
Cost: 800,000 DM.
Available through the German Embassy Film Library, Washington, D.C.

Satan's Brew (1975-76)
(Satansbraten)

Ce qui difference / les paiens de nous, / c'est qu'a l'origine / de toutes leurs croyances, / il y a un terrible effort / pour ne pas penser en hommes, / pour garder le contact / avec la creation entiere, / c'est-a-dire avec la divinite. —Antonin Artaud

Screenplay	Rainer Werner Fassbinder
Camera Operator	Jurgen Jurges (1. Phase), Michael Ballhaus
Editor	Thea Eymesz, Gabi Eichel
Sound	Paul Scholer, Rolf-Peter Notz, Roland Henschke
Music	Peer Raben
Set Design	Kurt Raab, Ulrike Bode
Assistant Director	Ila von Hasperg, Christa Reeh, Renate Leiffer
Producer	Michael Fengler
Production	Albatros Produktion, for Trio-Film

Cast: Kurt Raab (Walter Kranz), Margit Carstensen (Andree), Helen Vita (Luise Kranz), Volker Spengler (Ernst), Ingrid Caven (Lilly), Marquard Bohm (Rolf, her husband), Ulli Lommel (Lauf), Y Sa Lo (Lana), Katharina Buchhammer (Irmgart von Witzleben), Armin Meier (Stricher), Vitus Zeplichal (Urs), Dieter Schidǫr (Willy), Peter Chatel (Eugen), Michael Octave (young man), Katren Gebelein (Lilly's mother), Helmut Petigk (Schneider), Hannes Gromball (taxi driver), Adrian Hoven (doctor), Monika Teuber (woman in elevator.)

Filmed in 29 days in Munich in October, 1975 (14 days) and January-February, 1976 (15 days).
Running time, 112 mins.; 35 mm, color.
Cost: 600,000 DM.
Distributed in the U.S. by New Yorker Films.

Chinese Roulette (1976)
(Chineisisches Roulette)

Screenplay	Rainer Werner Fassbinder
Camera Operator	Michael Ballhaus
Editor	Ila von Hasperg, Juliane Lorenz
Sound	Roland Henschke
Music	Peer Raben
Set Design	Curd Melber
Assistant Director	Ila von Hasperg
Organization	Christian Hohoff, Harry Zottl, Kerstin Dobbertin
Producer	Michael Fengler
Production	Albatros Produktion, Munich/Les Films du Losange, Paris

Cast: Margit Carstensen (Ariane), Anna Karina (Irene), Alexander Allerson (Gerhard), Ulli Lommel (Kolbe), Andrea Schober (Angela), Mascha Meril (Traunitz), Brigitte Mira (Kast), Volker Spengler (Gabriel), Armin Meier (filling station attendant), Roland Henschke (beggar).

Filmed in 36 days Stockach (castle) and surroundings, Munich (airport) in April-June, 1976.
Running time, 86 mins.; 35 mm, color.
Cost: 1,100,000 DM.
Distributed in the U.S. by New Yorker Films.

Bolwieser (1976/77)

Screenplay	Rainer Werner Fassbinder (from the novel by Oskar Maria Graf).
Camera Operator	Michael Ballhaus
Editor	Ila von Hasperg, Juliane Lorenz
Sound	Reinhard Gloge
Music	Peer Raben
Set Design	Kurt Raab, Nico Kehrhan
Assistant Director	Christian Hohoff, Ila von Hasperg, Udo Kier
Costumes	Monika Altmann-Kriger
Production	Bavaria Atelier GmbH for Zweites Deutsches Fernsehen.

Cast: Kurt Raab (Xaver Ferdinand Maria Bolwieser, station master), Elisabeth Trissenaar (Hanni), Bernhard Helfrich (Frank Merkl, butcher and innkeeper), Udo Kier (Schafftaler, hairdresser), Volker Spengler (Mangst, secretary), Armin Meier (Scherber), Karl-Heinz von Hassel (Windegger), Gustl Maryhammer (Neidhart, Hanni's father), Maria Singer (Frau Neidhart), Willi Harlander (Stempflinger), Hannes Kaetner (Lederer), Gusti Kreissl (Frau Lederer), Helmut Alimonta (Hartmannseder), Peter Kern (Treuberger), Gottfried John (Finkelberger, lawyer), Gerhard Zwerenz (ferryman), Helmut Petigk (innkeeper), Sonja Neudorfer (innkeeper's wife), Monika Teuber (Mariele), Nino Korda (lawyer), Hannes Gromball (judge in district court), Alexander Allerson (chairman), Manfred Gunther (counsel for the defense), Roland Henschke (judge in Werburg), Adolph Gruber (accused peasant), Doris Mattes (witness), Ulrich Radke (Councellor Schneider), Liselotte Pempeit (Frau Kaser), Reinhard Weiser (sailor), Elma Karlowa (nurse), Isolde Barth (first heckler), Margot Mahler (second heckler), Renate Muhri (whore), Monica Gruber (waitress), Katharina Buchhammer (barmaid).

Filmed in 40 days on location Marxgrun Station (between Neila and Bad Steben) and other parts of Bavaria in October-December, 1976.
Running time, 104 mins., 20 secs. (I), 96 mins., 23 secs. (II); 16 mm, color.
Cost: 1,800,000 DM.
The shorter cinema version (about 120 min.) is available from the German Embassy Film Library, Washington, D.C.

Women in New York   (1977)
(Frauen in New York)

Television version of Rainer Werner Fassbinder's production for the German Playhouse in Hamburg.

Screenplay	Clare Booth: "The Women"/translated by Nora Gray
Camera Operator	Michael Ballhaus
Editor	Wolfgang Kerhutt
Sound	Horst Faahs
Set Design	Rolf Glittenberg
Costumes	Frieda Parmeggiani
TV adaptation	Dieter Meichsner
Production	Norddeutscher Rundfunk

Cast: Christa Berndl (Mary, Mrs. Stephen Haines), Margit Carstensen (Sylvia, Mrs. Howard Fowler), Anne-Marie Kuster (Peggy, Mrs. John Day), Eva Mattes (Edith, Mrs. Phelps Potter), Angela Schmid (Nancy Blake/Princess Tamara/Miss Trimmerback), Heide Grubl (Jane/gymnastics instructor, desperate girl), Ehmi Bessel (Mrs. Wagstaff/Ingrid, the cook/first directress/Miss Watts, secretary/second lady), Susanne Werth (first hairdresser, first saleswoman, first girl), Carola Schwarz (second hairdresser, second saleswoman/Helene, lady's maid), Irm Hermann (Olga, manicurist/Miriam), Adelheid Muther (Euphie/mannequin/cigarette girl), Ilse Bally (woman in mud pack/second directress/first lady), Andrea Grosske (Miss Fordyce, tutor/Luca, cleaning woman/Maggie, cook/widow), Christina Prior (little Mary), Gisela Uhlen (Mrs. Morehead/Comtesse de Lage), Barbara Sukowa (Crystal Allen), Henny Zschoppe (nurse), Sabine Wegener (debutante).

Filmed in 7 days in Hamburg in March, 1977.
Running time, 111 mins. 10 secs.; 16 mm, color.
Cost: 320,000 DM.

Despair (1977)
(Eine Reise ins Licht—Despair)

Dedicated to Antonin Artaud, Vincent van Gogh, Unica Zurn

Screenplay	Tom Stoppard (from the novel by Vladimir Nabokov
Camera Operator	Michael Ballhaus
Editor	Juliane Lorenz
Sound	James Willis
Music	Peer Raben
Set Design	Rolf Zehetbauer
Costumes	Dagmar Schauberger
Assistant Director	Harry Baer
Production	Peter Marthesheimer; NF Geria II Film GmbH, Munich, in collaboration with SFP, Paris, produced by Bavaria Atelier GmbH.

Cast: Dirk Bogarde (Hermann Hermann), Andrea Ferreol (Lydia), Volker Spengler (Ardalion), Klaus Lowitsch (Felix), Alexander Allerson (Mayer), Bernhard Wicki (Orlovius), Peter Kern (Muller), Gottfried John (Perebrodov), Adrian Hoven (Inspector Schelling), Roger Fritz (Inspector Braun), Hark Bohm (doctor), Y Sa Lo (Elsie), Liselotte Eder (secretary), Armin Meier (foreman).

Filmed in 41 days on location in Munich, Interlaken, Berlin, Lubeck, Braunschweig, Hamburg, Molln in April-June, 1977.
Running time, 119 mins.; 35 mm, color.
Cost: 6,000,000 DM.
Distributed in the U.S. by New Line.

244

Germany in Autumn   (1977/78)
(Deutschland im Herbst)

Directed by—Alf Brustellin, Rainer Werner Fassbinder, Alexander Kluge, Maximiliane Mainka, Edgar Reitz, Katja Rupe/Hans Peter Cloos, Volker Schlondorff, Bernhard Sinkel.

Screenplay	Heinrich Boll, Peter Steinbach, the directors
Camera Operator	Michael Ballhaus (Fassbinder episode), Jurgen Jurges, Bodo Kessler, Dietrich Lohmann, Colin Mounier, Jorg Schmidt-Reitwein
Editor	Heidi Genee, Mulle Goetz-Dickopp, Juliane Lorenz (Fassbinder episode), Beate Mainka-Jellinghaus, Tanja Schmidbauer, Christina Warnck
Sound	Roland Henschke (Fassbinder episode), Martin Muller, Gunter Stadelmann
Set Design	Henning von Gierke, Winfried Hennig, Toni Ludi
Production Coordinators	Heinz Badewitz, Karl Helmer, Herbert Kerz
Production	Pro-ject Film Production, Filmverlag der Autoren/Hallelujah-Film/Kairos-Film

Collaborators: Wolfgang Baechler, Heinz Bennent, Wolf Biermann, Joachim Bissmeyer, Caroline Chaniolleau, Hans Peter Cloos, Otto Friebel, Hildegard Friese, Michael Gahr, Vadim Glowna, Helmut Griem, Horatius Haeberle, Hannelore Hoger, Petra Kiener, Dieter Laser, Horst Mahler, Lisi Mangold, Eva Meier, Enno Patalas, Werner Possardt, Franz Priegel, Leon Rainer, Katja Rupe, Walter Schmiedinger, Gerhard Schneider, Corinna Spies, Eric Vilgertshofer, Franziska Walser, Angela Winkler, Manfred Zapatka, the "Rote Rube" collective; in the Fassbinder episode: Rainer Werner Fassbiner, Liselotte Eder, Armin Meier.

Filmed in 6 days in various parts of West Germany (Fassbinder episode in his Munich apartment) in October, 1977-February, 1978.
Running time, 124 mins.; Fassbinder episode: 26 mins., 20 secs.; 35 mm, color and B&W.
Cost: 450,000 DM.
Distributed in the U.S. by New Line.

The Marriage of Maria Braun   (1978)
(Die Ehe der Maria Braun)

For Peter Zadek

Screenplay	Peter Marthesheimer, Pea Frohlich, from an idea by Rainer Werner Fassbinder
Camera Operator	Michael Ballhaus
Editor	Juliane Lorenz
Sound	Jim Willis
Music	Peer Raben
Set Design	Helga Ballhaus
Set Construction	Norbert Scherer
Costumes	Barbara Baum
Assistant Director	Rolf Buhrmann
Production	Michael Fengler; Albatros Produktion

Cast: Hanna Schygulla (Maria), Klaus Lowitsch (Hermann), Ivan Desny (Oswald), Gottfried John (Willi), Gisela Uhlen (Maria's mother), Gunter Lamprecht (Wetzel), George Byrd (Bill), Elisabeth Trissenaar (Betti), Isolde Barth (Vevi), Peter Berling (Bronski), Sonja Neuforfer (Red Cross nurse), Liselotte Eder (Frau Ehmke), Volker Spengler (Schaffner), Karl-Heinz von Hassel (District Attorney), Michael Ballhaus (lawyer), Christine Hopf-de Loup (notary), Hark Bohm (Senkenberg), Dr. Horst-Dieter Klock (man with car), Gunther Kaufmann (friend in car), Bruce Low (friend at conference), Rainer Werner Fassbinder (black marketeer), Claus Holm (doctor), Anton Schirsner (Grandpa Berger), Hannes Kaetner (registrar), Martin Haussler (reporter), Norbert Scherer (waiter I), Rolf Buhrmann (waiter II), Arthur Glogau (waiter III).

Filmed in 35 days Coburg and Berlin in January-March, 1978.
Running time, 120 mins.; 35 mm, color.
Cost: 1,975,000 DM.
Distributed in the U.S. by New Yorker Films.

In a Year of 13 Moons   (1978)
(In einem Jahr mit 13 Monden)

Screenplay	Rainer Werner Fassbinder
Camera Operator	Rainer Werner Fassbinder
Editor	Rainer Werner Fassbinder
Camera Assistant	Werner Luring
Sound and Lighting	Karl Scheidt, Wolfgang Mund
Sets	Franz Vacek
Production Manager	Isolde Barth
	with the assistance of Milan Bor, Walter Bockmayer, Jo Braun, Juliane Lorenz, Peer Raben, Volker Spengler, Alexander Witt.
Production	Tango Film/Pro-ject Film Production, Filmverlag der Autoren

Cast: Volker Spengler (Elvira Weishaupt), Ingrid Caven ("Red" Zora), Gottfried John (Anton Seitz), Elisabeth Trissenaar (Irene), Eva Mattes (Marie-Ann), Gunther Kaufmann (chauffeur), Liselotte Pempeit (Sister Gudrun), Isolde Barth (Sybille), Karl Scheidt (Hacker), Walter Bockmayer ("Soul" Frieda), Peter Kollek (drunk), Bob Dorsay (vagrant), Gunther Holzapfel (Seitz's bodyguard), Ursula Lillig (cleaning woman), Gerhard Zwerenz (Burghard Hauer, journalist).

Filmed in 25 days on location in Frankfurt am Main in July-August, 1978.
Running time, 124 mins.; 35 mm, color.
Cost: 700,000 DM.
Distributed in the U.S. by New Yorker Films.

The Third Generation   (1978/79)
(Die dritte Generation)

Screenplay	Rainer Werner Fassbinder
Camera Operator	Rainer Werner Fassbinder
Editor	Juliane Lorenz
Sound	Milan Bor, Jean Luc Marie
Music	Peer Raben
Set Design	Raul Gimenez, Volker Spengler
Technical Assistants	Ekkehard Heinrich, Hans Bucking
Production Manager	Harry Baer
Assistant Director	Diana Elephant
Production	Tango Film/Pro-ject Film Production, Filmverlag der Autoren

Cast: Volker Spengler (August Brem), Bulle Ogier (Hilde Krieger), Hanna Schygulla (Susanne Gast), Harry Baer (Rudolf Mann), Vitus Zeplichal (Bernhard von Stein), Udo Kier (Edgar Gast), Margit Carstensen (Petra Vielhaber), Gunther Kaufmann (Franz Walsch), Eddie Constantine (Peter Lenz), Raul Gimenez (Paul), Y Sa Lo (Ilse Neumann), Hark Bohm (Gerhard Gast), Claus Holm (Grandfather Gast), Lilo Peimpeit (Mother Gast), Jurgen Draeger (Hans Vielhaber).

Filmed in 30 days on location in Berlin in December, 1978 - January, 1979. Running time, 110 mins.; 35 mm, color.
Cost: 800,000 DM.
Distributed in the U.S. by New Yorker Films.

Berlin Alexanderplatz   (1979-80)

Screenplay	Rainer Werner Fassbinder (from a novel by Alfred Doblin)
Camera Operator	Xaver Schwarzenberger
Editor	Juliane Lorenz
Music	Peer Raben
Sound	Carsten Ullrich
Set Design	Helmut Gassner, Werner Achmann
Costumes	Barbara Baum
Production Manager	Dieter Minx
Producer	Peter Marthesheimer; Bavaria Atelier GmbH, Italian Television Network in collaboration with Westdeutscher Rundfunk

Cast: Gunter Lamprecht (Franz Biberkopf), Barbara Sukawa (Mieze), Gottfried John (Reinhold), Barbara Valentin (Ida), Hanna Schygulla, Franz Buchreiser, Claus Holm, Brigitte Mira, Roger Fritz, Hark Bohm, Ivan Desny, Annemarie Duringer, Elisabeth Trissenaar, Helen Vita, Herbert Steinmetz, Gerhard Zwerenz.

Filmed in 154 days from June 1979 to April 1980.
Running time, 15½ hours; aired on television in 14 parts.
Cost: 13,000,000 DM.

Lili Marleen   (1980)

Screenplay	Manfried Purzer (in collaboration with Joshua Sinclair and R.W. Fassbinder, from Lale Andererson's autobiography, *Der Himmel hat viele Farben.*
Camera Operator	Xaver Schwarzenberger
Artistic Assistant	Harry Baer
Music	Peer Raben
Set Design	Rolf Zehetbauer
Production Manager	Konsantin Torsch-Thoeren
Producer	Luggi Waldleitner, in association with Enzo Peri, Roxy-Rialto-Lex Film (Munich)

Cast: Hanna Schygulla (Willie), Giancarlo Giannini (Robert), Mel Ferrer (David Mendelsson), Karl Heinz von Hassel (Henkel), Hark Bohm (Taschner), Erik Schumann, Gottfried John, Karin Baal, Christine Kaufmann, Udo Kier, Roger Fritz, Rainer Will, Raul Gimenez, Adrian Hoven, Willy Harlander, Barbara Valentin, Helen Vita, Elisabeth Volksman, Lilo Pempeit, Traute Hass, Brigitte Mira, Herb Andress, Michael McLernon, Jurgen Drager, Rudolf Lenz, Toni Nelzle, Irm Hermann.

Filmed in 47 days in July through September 1980.
Running time, 120 mins.; 35 mm, color.
Cost: 10,500,000 DM.
Distributed in the U.S. by United Artists Classics.

LIBRARY
ST. LOUIS COMMUNITY COLLEGE
AT FLORISSANT VALLEY

INVENTORY 1983